MODERN POETRY
of Western America

An anthology
edited by

Clinton F. Larson
Professor of English and
Poet in Residence,
Brigham Young University

William Stafford
Professor of English,
Lewis and Clark College

Brigham Young University Press
Provo, Utah

Library of Congress Cataloging in Publication Data
Main entry under title:

Modern poetry of Western America

    1. American poetry—The West.   2. American po-
etry—20th century.   3. The West—Poetry.   I. Lar-
son, Clinton F.   II. Stafford, William Edgar,
1914-
PS561.M6   811'.5'408   75-8697
ISBN 0-8425-0423-0
ISBN 0-8425-0424-9 pbk.

Library of Congress Catalog Card Number: 75-8697

International Standard Book Number: 0-8425-0423-0 (cloth)
                                     0-8425-0424-9 (paper)
Brigham Young University Press, Provo, Utah 84602
©1975 Brigham Young University Press. All rights reserved.
Printed in the United States of America
75 4500p 500c 7500

Copyrights and Acknowledgments

Birney, Earle. "There Are Delicacies," from *Rag and Bone Shop;* "The Bear on the Delhi Road," "Biography," "Bushed," "El Greco: Espolio," "Irapuato," "Looking from Oregon," "Man Is a Snow," "Song for Sunsets," "War Winters," "Wind-Chimes in a Temple Ruin," from *Collected Poems* by Earle Birney, reprinted by permission of The Canadian Publishers, McClelland and Stewart Limited, Toronto.

Cunningham, James V. "The Phoenix," "Consolatio Nova," from *Collected Poems and Epigrams of J. V. Cunningham* ©1971 by J. V. Cunningham, reprinted by permission of the Swallow Press, Inc.

DeFrees, Madeline. "In the Scales: I," "In the Scales: II," reprinted from *The Literary Review* (Summer 1966, Volume IX, Number 4), published by Farleigh Dickinson University, Rutherford, N.J.; "Hope Diamonds," "With a Bottle of Blue Nun to All My Friends," from *The American Review*, reprinted by permission of the author; "My Dream of Pure Invention," from *The Nation*, November 19, 1973, reprinted by permission of the publisher; "Watch for Fallen Rock," reprinted by permission of the *Garfield Lake Review*, Olivet, Michigan.

Ferril, Thomas Hornsby. "Lens for Plum Blossom," "Noon," "The Prairie Melts," "Wood," from *New and Selected Poems,* Harper and Brothers, 1952, reprinted by permission of the author; "Swallows," from *Words for Denver,* William Morrow and Company, 1966, reprinted by permission of the author.

Ghiselin, Brewster. "Love Letter," "The Catch," "Marlin," "Vantage," "Light," from *Country of the Minotaur,* by Brewster Ghiselin, copyright ©1965, 1969, 1970 by Brewster Ghiselin; "Song at San Carlos Bay," from *The Michigan Quarterly Review* 13(Spring 1974): 99-101, ©1974 University of Michigan.

Gunn, Thom. "In Santa Maria Del Popolo," "Considering the Snail," reprinted with the permission of Farrar, Straus and Giroux, Inc., from *Moly* and *My Sad Captains* by Thom Gunn, copyright ©1961, 1971, 1973 by Thom Gunn.

Haines, John. "Leaves and Ashes," "The Weaver," "The Calendar," from *Leaves and Ashes,* Kayak Press and West Coast Poetry Review, 1974, reprinted by permission of the author.

Hanson, Kenneth. "Snow," "Before the Storm," "The Distance Anywhere," "The Divide," "Montana," "First of All," from *Poetry Northwest,* reprinted by permission of the author and *Poetry Northwest;* "Elegiac," from *Sewanee Review* 67:3(Summer 1959), reprinted by permission of the author.

Harris, John. "Hay Derrick," "Tag, I.D.," from *Barbed Wire* ©1973 Brigham Young University Press, reprinted by permission of the publishers.

Hugo, Richard. "Duwamish," "At the Stilli's Mouth," reprinted by permission of the author; "Indian Graves at Jocko," "Bear Paw," "Driving Montana," from *The Lady in Kicking Horse Reservoir,* poems by Richard Hugo, reprinted by permission of W. W. Norton and Company, Inc., copyright ©1973 by Richard Hugo.

Inada, Lawson. "Asian Brother, Asian Sister," from *Roots: An Asian American Reader,* Franklin S. Odo, editor, the Regents of the University of California, 1971, reprinted by permission of the author.

Jeffers, Robinson. "Birds," copyright 1925 and renewed 1953 by Robinson Jeffers, reprinted from *The Selected Poetry of Robinson Jeffers,* by permission of Random House, Inc.; "Science," copyright 1925 and renewed 1953 by Robinson Jeffers, reprinted from *The Selected Poetry of Robinson Jeffers,* by permission of Random House, Inc; "To the Stone-Cutters," copyright 1924 and renewed 1952 by Robinson Jeffers, reprinted from *The Selected Poetry of Robinson Jeffers,* by permission of Random House, Inc.; "A Flight of Swans," copyright 1935 and renewed 1963 by Donnan Jeffers and Garth Jeffers, reprinted from *The Selected Poetry of Robinson Jeffers,* by permission of Random House, Inc.; "Original Sin," copyright 1948 by Robinson Jeffers, reprinted from *Selected Poems,* by Robinson Jeffers by permission of Random House, Inc.; "Credo," reprinted by permission of Donnan C. Jeffers, Jeffers literary properties, Carmel, California.

Larson, Clinton F. "Homestead in Idaho," "To a Dying Girl," "Advent," from *Lord of Experience,* Brigham Young University Press, 1965, reprinted by permission of the author; "Seven-tenths of a Second," "Cactus Stem," from *Counterpoint,* Brigham Young University Press, 1974, reprinted by permission of the author.

Levine, Philip. "A New Day," by Philip Levine. Copyright 1965 by Philip Levine. Reprinted from *Not This Pig,* by Philip Levine, by permission of Wesleyan University Press. "Clouds," by Philip Levine. From *Red Dust,* Kayak Books, © 1971, reprinted by permission of the author. "Detroit Grease Shop Poem," and "Breath," from *They Feed They Lion* by Philip Levine. "Detroit Grease Shop Poem" appeared originally in *Unicorn Folio,* reprinted by permission of Atheneum Publishers.

Lueders, Edward. "Rodeo," by Edward Lueders from *Reflections on a Gift of Watermelon Pickle...* by Stephen Dunning, Edward Lueders, and Hugh Smith, copyright ©1966, by Scott, Foresman and Company; "A Tour of the Southwest," from *New Mexico Quarterly* 13:1(Spring 1963): 32, reprinted by permission of the author; "The Man in Overalls," first published in *Images and Impressions,* reprinted by permission of the author.

McPherson, Sandra. "Elegies for the Hot Season," "Preparation," reprinted from *Elegies for the Hot Season* by Sandra McPherson, copyright ©1970 by Indiana University Press, Bloomington, reprinted by permission of the publisher; "Wearing White," copyright 1973 by *Harper's Magazine,* reprinted from the July 1973 issue by special permission.

To Ezra Pound of Hailey
and Robert Frost of San Francisco

Contents

ix

xiv

Foreword

The savor of life is always particular, determined for every individual by the quality of his being and by the nature of the interplay between what he is and whatever world he moves in. It is a truism that, no matter how completely we may be engaged in the communion of humanity, we are all somewhat different from one another. But that we differ in more than individual ways, by necessity of many influences of place and time and the actions these engender, is perhaps not sufficiently appreciated. The order of human behavior is less like the drift of logs inert in the steady flux of a flume than like the choreography of trout in different parts of the stream. A Westerner reading the poetry collected in this anthology would probably feel differently about some of it than an Easterner—or than a Southerner—confirmed in adaptation, and perhaps allegiance, to the region of his choice and the ways of life it proposes. Not provincialism, but the inevitable emphasis we experience in one order of life or another, orients each of us, writer and reader alike, to the sphere of his most immediate, intimate, and vital activity, the enclave and focus in which his interests and passions develop and flourish.

Some of the poets represented in this anthology are cosmopolitan in fact of experience, as well as of mind and spirit. Not all are Western in origin, and many have spent much time in other parts of the world. Yet all are Western in the sense that throughout years of intimate encounter the West has enriched and shaped their awareness. It has brought into their poetry substance and realizations provided by the life and landscape of the region, its people, animals, and vegetation, its earth and waters and air and lighting, its weather in all seasons, its moods, its atmosphere in every sense of the word. In some measure, and in various ways, the very breath of these poems has been disciplined by that atmosphere.

Reading them in the light of the vision they define and sharing in the energy that moves them, all—including Westerners themselves—may enlarge their understanding and appreciation of a region so diverse in its aspects and in the modes of life it supports that coming to know it very fully must require years, as well as extraordinary opportunities. Poetry is an instrument of knowledge. And yet it is not an appropriate or effectual means of disseminating sheer information. It does not lend its power to exploitation of subject matter in the manner of some so-called regional writing. In any mature work, local color is incidental. As it is immerged in the whole, without loss of visibility its look of peculiarity disappears like that of any familiar thing in the environment. Many of the poems in this anthology do not deal with the West at all, and none of them are designed for display of the characteristics of the region that has nourished the poets. They are illustrative of its character almost in the same sense that the flora of a region may show the qualities of the earth from which it springs and of the weather that fosters the integral and autonomous life that has taken shape and gathered strength for flowering there.

Brewster Ghiselin

Preface

The publication of *Modern Poetry of Western America* implies that the West is developing a "regional" literature which not only expresses the meaning of life in the West but comfortably joins the general progress of twentieth-century American literature. The progress of scholarship in the earlier literature of the West is firm and distinguished, as evidenced by publications, seminars, and conferences which have defined, or helped to define, ethnic and subregional literatures, problems of social and religious influence, the rise of formulated "western stories" from distinguished precedents, local colorism, folklore, and other classifications that seem at home with Western themes. But since the early thirties, and even before, the poets of the West, in company with novelists, playwrights, and other creative artists, have acquired a more universal sense and responsibility, along with a desire to express themselves in a variety of styles and forms.

Many western poets, among them Earle Birney, Brewster Ghiselin, and Thomas Hornsby Ferril, have implicitly emulated the earlier successes of Ezra Pound and Robinson Jeffers. A number of poets have become widely recognized and appreciated through prize-winning poetry in such magazines as *The Sewanee Review, The New Yorker, Poetry, The Atlantic Monthly,* and *The Hudson Review.* And their work is contained in anthologies which have suggested the scope of the literature of the West, such as Ray B. West's *Rocky Mountain Reader.*

In 1972, when Anthony Ostroff visited Brigham Young University, Clinton Larson discussed the idea of the anthology with him. Ostroff suggested William Stafford as coeditor. Stafford accepted, the idea being that he would collect poetry from poets on the west coast and that Larson would collect poetry from inland poets, with a provision for much interchange of critical opinion between them.

As the editors began, it soon became apparent that the volume of good modern poetry in the West had become so large that to represent all the fine poets in a single book would not be financially feasible. It then became the editors' task to select a range of poets whose work has received substantial critical acknowledgment and praise. This book is intended to present the best from these poets, and the editors hope it will provide a setting by which the breadth of the poets' regionalism can be seen and appreciated.

The editors invited the living poets represented in this volume to submit up to four hundred lines each for consideration. Poems of deceased poets were selected on the basis of critical acclaim and variety. A winnowing process began in which the editors isolated poems which seemed to them to have enduring quality in terms of artistic competence and universality of appeal. The editorial committee of Brigham Young University were most helpful in offering suggestions and initially approving the anthology for publication. The manuscript was then sent to reviewers who suggested additions and deletions, and certain revisions of this preface, in order to make the whole presentation more acceptable and useful.

Modern Poetry of Western America is intended for the general reader as well as for those who might want to use it in the classroom. It includes poetry as varied as the landscape itself and ranges far beyond it, into international subjects and moods and into the experiences of the disciplines of the spirit and mind. Brewster Ghiselin perceives the fauna of the West with meaningful precision and feeling. Robinson Jeffers, through long, sinuous lines, conveys the expanse and brilliance of the scenery of the California coast. The teeming social poetry of Ginsberg and Ferlinghetti began with protest, then developed into a poetry of epiphany which expresses an expansive variety of philosophies and religious insights. Zen Buddhism has had far-ranging effects upon many San Francisco poets. The transcendental sense of its tenets is found in Gary Snyder's poems about pioneer and Indian folklore, in which animism, in its possibilities for ethnic expression, becomes amazingly negotiable. Ann Stanford conjures so expertly that a swarm of bees seems companionable. Karl Shapiro demonstrates a profound ability to convey insight in poems in which abstract words are used to accumulate the power of concrete experience. In this volume there are poems based on experiences in science and technology and the milieu of the megalopolis. Ecological poems abound, as well as poems of social protest that convey the tenor of "subcultures," including the Indian and Chicano. Some poets have emulated the aesthetic experimentations of Pound, Eliot, Jeffers, and Roethke. Thomas Hornsby Ferril combines the sense of the Old West with a Whitmanesque enjoyment for the new.

In its variety, the regionalism of the poetry of the West is commendably not self-conscious. Even the religious poetry of the Mormon people, based as it is upon a firm eschatology, is not overtly symbolic, but rather derives from the most fundamental experiences of "making the desert blossom as a rose," and the Mormon people themselves do not customarily think of religious symbols as symbols only, but also as direct expressions of religious experience.

The western frontier of the nineteenth century is amply discussed by literary and social historians and by folklorists, but since its disappearance as a literal reality it has remained evanescent in the minds of many, particularly in the minds of the poets. In the perceptions of Keith Wilson and A. Wilber Stevens, for example, the landscape remains vivid, even stark, and gains the sense of an ambient myth, a reality which imposes disciplined habits of mind and sharpens the senses to animallike alertness. Like myth, it seems to elude scientific inquiry and is richest when perceived in metaphysical communion. It functions as an extension of man's Being, and some have averred that it can be expressed only in poetry. Much of the poetry in which images of the landscape appear conveys an aura of revelation, through which western poetry gains a kind of unity. Geographical boundaries, such as an oval that might be drawn on a map from Vancouver to Snoqualmie Pass, Cour d'Alene, Jackson, North Platte, Denver, Tucson, San Diego, San Francisco, Coos Bay, and back to Vancouver, can be only ancillary to the interest that the poets themselves have in western America, though it is true that the editors, in extending their invitations, had such an area in mind.

Analogical truth which finds its source in the western landscape denies posturing, speciousness, or the tacit lie; it affirms sensibility, consistency, and good faith. It offers perspective through beauty and primitivistic insight. But people are often afraid of western poetry because it thrives even in such social conditions as we know now surround us; we nevertheless recognize that in the flux of things it can enable us to create in our lives a greater order than we might otherwise perceive as possible. But that order cannot be hastened into being. We cannot see the stars until it gets dark enough to see them, but we can watch them flicker on and then form the constellations. We must be willing to wait upon them, hoping that the atmosphere is clear enough for patterns to appear.

We have swung a loop that reaches back for poets who were still writing in the 1960s—and forward for the best work of poets who were born in the 1940s. Robinson Jeffers and Theodore Roethke—national and international figures—give a firm base for the gathering of the early work of moderns. A glance at the sequence of poets—presented chronologically—will show persons whose work is just beginning to be noted by the general public; but no one volume could have the scope of this one in time and space and also include the host of lively talents now arriving on the scene. This book is intended to show work of persons who have established themselves clearly in the consciousness of those who follow current western literature.

A mixture of opportunities and limits has shaped this collection. We have followed the poets' suggestions, but have also acted independently to capture variety and representation. Often faced with coercive advice about writers and poems treasured in a certain locality, we occasionally have had to leave out impressive talents in order to have room for representative writers from another area or of another stripe.

Early in this work, through a chance friendship and then an enterprise that began with convergent interests in literature, it became clear to us that publication of this anthology might bring together several cultural and ethnic groups in the West who are sometimes through historical accident separated and thus deprived. Through the common interests of the editors and the cooperation of the BYU Press, this book yokes together for good the converging sweep of talents at large over the West. We explicitly recognize this opportunity and embrace it.

We have felt just as purposeful about other divisions in the culture of the West, but often with less effect. Surely literature of the area should relate significantly to peoples native to it. For these people—Indians and Eskimoes—poetry was apparently once a greater element than it is for any of those now living. And the Spanish-speaking people, and those whose ancestors lived in Asia, or Africa—all of these carry significant values into the life now lived throughout the West. Wherever these values surface in the language of poetry, they deserve a place in a collection like this; and we have felt wistful about the search to do justice to influences which have recently become more vigorous and more recognized. We are not satisfied with our efforts; we have been baffled, like many others trying to make the reach. Poetry, of all forms of discourse, depends on a fluency in the language of writer and reader alike: the syllables have to help, and the readers have to be ready. Language in poetry won't be a slave; it has to be a friend.

But this collection does its best to range the area, the culture, and the language. We thank those who provided poems and those who lavished advice while we struggled through the tangle of opportunities and limits toward this actualization.

Clinton F. Larson
William Stafford

Robinson Jeffers
(1887-1962)

BIRDS

The fierce musical cries of a couple of sparrowhawks hunting on the head-
land,
Hovering and darting, their heads northwestward,
Prick like silver arrows shot through a curtain the noise of the ocean
Trampling its granite; their red backs gleam
Under my window around the stone corners; nothing gracefuller, nothing
Nimbler in the wind. Westward the wave-gleaners,
The old gray sea-going gulls are gathered together, the northwest wind
wakening
Their wings to the wild spirals of the wind-dance.
Fresh as the air, salt as the foam, play birds in the bright wind, fly falcons
Forgetting the oak and the pinewood, come gulls
From the Carmel sands and the sands at the river-mouth, from Lobos and out
of the limitless
Power of the mass of the sea, for a poem
Needs multitude, multitudes of thoughts, all fierce, all flesh-eaters, musically
clamorous
Bright hawks that hover and dart headlong, and ungainly
Gray hungers fledged with desire of transgression, salt slimed beaks, from the
sharp
Rock-shores of the world and the secret waters.

SCIENCE

Man, introverted man, having crossed
In passage and but a little with the nature of things this latter century
Has begot giants; but being taken up
Like a maniac with self-love and inward conflicts cannot manage his hybrids.
Being used to deal with edgeless dreams,
Now he's bred knives on nature turns them also inward: they have thirsty
points though.
His mind forebodes his own destruction;
Actæon who saw the goddess naked among leaves and his hounds tore him.
A little knowledge, a pebble from the shingle,
A drop from the oceans: who would have dreamed this infinitely little too
much?

1

TO THE STONE-CUTTERS

Stone-cutters fighting time with marble, you foredefeated
Challengers of oblivion
Eat cynical earnings, knowing rock splits, records fall down,
The square-limbed Roman letters
Scale in the thaws, wear in the rain. The poet as well
Builds his monument mockingly;
For man will be blotted out, the blithe earth die, the brave sun
Die blind and blacken to the heart:
Yet stones have stood for a thousand years, and pained thoughts found
The honey of peace in old poems.

FLIGHT OF SWANS

One who sees giant Orion, the torches of winter midnight,
Enormously walking above the ocean in the west of heaven;
And watches the track of this age of time at its peak of flight
Waver like a spent rocket, wavering toward new discoveries,
Mortal examinations of darkness, soundings of depth;
And watches the long coast mountain vibrate from bronze to green,
Bronze to green, year after year, and all the streams
Dry and flooded, dry and flooded, in the racing seasons;
And knows that exactly this and not another is the world,
The ideal is phantoms for bait, the spirit is a flicker on a grave;—
May serve, with a certain detachment, the fugitive human race,
Or his own people, or his own household; but hardly himself;
And will not wind himself into hopes nor sicken with despairs.
He has found the peace and adored the God; he handles in autumn
The germs of far-future spring.
                              Sad sons of the stormy fall,
No escape, you have to inflict and endure; surely it is time for you
To learn to touch the diamond within to the diamond outside,
Thinning your humanity a little between the invulnerable diamonds,
Knowing that your angry choices and hopes and terrors are in vain,
But life and death not in vain; and the world is like a flight of swans.

ORIGINAL SIN

The man-brained and man-handed ground-ape, physically
The most repulsive of all hot-blooded animals
Up to that time of the world: they had dug a pitfall
And caught a mammoth, but how could their sticks and stones
Reach the life in that hide? They danced around the pit, shrieking
With ape excitement, flinging sharp flints in vain, and the stench of their
    bodies
Stained the white air of dawn; but presently one of them
Remembered the yellow dancer, wood-eating fire
That guards the cave-mouth; he ran and fetched him, and others
Gathered sticks at the wood's edge; they made a blaze
And pushed it into the pit, and they fed it high, around the mired sides
Of their huge prey. They watched the long hairy trunk
Waver over the stifle-trumpeting pain,
And they were happy.

      Meanwhile the intense color and nobility of sunrise,
Rose and gold and amber, flowed up the sky. Wet rocks were shining, a little
    wind
Stirred the leaves of the forest and the marsh flag-flowers; the soft valley
    between the low hills
Became as beautiful as the sky; while in its midst, hour after hour, the happy
    hunters
Roasted their living meat slowly to death.

                            These are the people.
This is the human dawn. As for me, I would rather
Be a worm in a wild apple than a son of man.
But we are what we are, and we might remember
Not to hate any person, for all are vicious.
And not to be astonished at any evil, all are deserved;
And not to fear death: it is the only way to be cleansed.

CREDO

My friend from Asia has powers and magic, he plucks a blue leaf from the
    young blue-gum
And gazing upon it, gathering and quieting
The God in his mind, creates an ocean more real than the ocean, the salt, the
    actual
Appalling presence, the power of the waters.
He believes that nothing is real except as we make it.
                                   I humbler have found in my blood
Bred west of Caucasus a harder mysticism.
Multitude stands in my mind but I think that the ocean in the bone vault is
    only
The bone vault's ocean: out there is the ocean's;
The water is the water, the cliff is the rock, come shocks and flashes of
    reality. The mind
Passes, the eye closes, the spirit is a passage:
The beauty of things was born before eyes and sufficient to itself: the heart-
    breaking beauty
Will remain when there is no heart to break for it.

Thomas Hornsby Ferril
(1896-   )

LENS FOR PLUM BLOSSOM

From tree to tree ahead of me
   A thousand blackbirds flutter.
Then wheel their wings in synchrony
   Like blades of a window shutter.

Blackbirds open, blackbirds close
   The snowy woods: my steaming horse
Is breathing frost and swings his nose
   Up the frozen watercourse.

Sundown notches the mountain gap,
   I snatch a twig of cottonwood,
I stare at the sun through amber sap
   That droops from an icy bud.

It isn't like a lens of glass,
   Nothing that I see is clear:
Blur of bud and mountain pass
   Over a horse's ear.

Yet staring so, not budged an inch,
   I feel the white plum blossoms come
To blow against the saddle cinch
   Shuddering winter-numb.

NOON

Noon is half the passion of light,
Noon is the middle prairie and the slumber,
The lull of resin weed, the yucca languor,
The wilt of sage at noon is the longest distance
    any nostril knows . . .
How far have we come to feel the shade of this tree?

SWALLOWS

The prairie wind blew harder than it could,
Even the spines of cactus trembled back,
I crouched in an arroyo clamping my hands
On my eyes the sand was stinging yellow black.

In the break of the black I let my lashes part,
Looked overhead and saw I was not alone,
I could almost reach through the roar and almost touch
A treadmill of swallows almost holding their own.

THE PRAIRIE MELTS

The prairie melts into the throats of larks
And green like water green begins to flow
Into the pinto patches of the snow.

I'm here, I move my foot, I count the mountains:
I can make calculations of my being
Here in the spring again, feeling it, seeing . . .

Three granite mountain ranges wore away
While I was coming here, that is the fourth
To shine in spring to sunlight from the north.

A mountain range ago the sea was here,
Now I am here, the falcons floating over,
Bluebirds swimming foredeeps of the blue,
Spindrift magpies black and splashing white,
The winged fins, the birds, the water green . . .

Not ocean ever now but lilies here,
Sand lilies, yucca lilies water-petaled,
Lilies too delicate, only a little while,
Lilies like going away, like a far sound,
Lilies like wanting to be loved
And tapping with a stick,
An old man tapping
The world in springtime with a stick.

This buffalo grass? O, you who are not here,
What if I knock upon your tombs and say:
The grass is back! Why are you still away?

I know the myth for spring I used to know:
The Son of God was pinned to a wooden truss
But lived again, His blood contiguous

To mine, His blood still ticking like a clock
Against the collar of my overcoat
That I have buttoned tight to warm my throat.

Who was His lover? That might keep Him nearer.
Whom did He love in springtime fingering
All fruit to come in any blossom white?
Cupping His hand for tips of nakedness
And whispering:

"You are the flowers, Beloved,
You are the footstep in the darkness always,
You are the first beginning of forever,
The first fire, the wash of it, the light,
The sweetest plume of wind for a walled town"?

I light my pipe. A heavy gopher sags
Into her burrow scarfed with striping snow,
So quick, so slow, I hardly see her go.

Yonder, a barbed-wire fence, and I remember
Without intention how a wire can twist
A gopher hole until it burns the wrist . . .

7

And there are wrists like mine that hang in trees,
And overcoats like mine to mulch the stubble,
And there are houses where the young men say
It would be different if the harbors and
The looms were ours . . .
The end of women wailing for a ship.

But sundown changes day to yesterday:
The purple light withdraws from purple light,
The listing mountains close the lilies tight.

Above the blackness still one falcon burns,
So high, so pale, the palest star seems nearer,
One fleck of sun, one atom-floating mirror.

His shadow will not strike this world tonight:
There is a darker homing hollow bone
Of wings returning gives to wings unknown.

My tilted skull? My socket eyes? Are these
With chalk of steers apprenticed to the grass
When mountains wear away and falcons pass?

No answer is.
                    No policy of rock
Or angel speaks.
                    Yet there could come a child
A long time hence at sundown to this prairie,
A child far-generated, lover to lover,
Lover to lover, lover to lover over . . .
(O I can hear them coming, hear them speaking
Far as the pale arroyos of the moon.)

The child could walk this prairie where I stand,
Seeing the sundown spokes of purple turning,
The child could whisper to a falcon floating:
"I am not lost.
                    They told me of this prairie:
This is the prairie where they used to come
To watch the lilies and to watch the falcons."

WOOD

There was a dark and awful wood
Where increments of death accrued
To every leaf and antlered head
Until it withered and was dead,
And lonely there I wandered
And wandered and wandered.

But once a myth-white moon shone there
And you were kneeling by a flower,
And it was practical and wise
For me to kneel and you to rise,
And me to rise and turn to go,
And you to turn and whisper *no,*
And seven wondrous stags that I
Could not believe walked slowly by.

Ivor Winters
(1900-1968)

JOHN DAY, FRONTIERSMAN

Among the first and farthest! Elk and deer
Fell as your rifle rang in rocky caves;
There your lean shadow swept the still frontier,
Your eyes regarded the Columbia's waves.

Amid the stony winter, gray with care,
Hunted by savages from sleep to sleep
—Those patriots of darkness and despair!—
You climbed in solitude what rigid steep!

Broken at last by very force of frame,
By wintry hunger like a warrior's brand,
You died a madman. And now bears your name
A gentle river in a fertile land.

The eminence is gone that met your eye;
The winding savage, too, has sunk away.
Now, like a summer myth, the meadows lie,
Deep in the calm of silvan slow decay.

JOHN SUTTER

I was the patriarch of the shining land,
Of the blond summer and metallic grain;
Men vanished at the motion of my hand,
And when I beckoned they would come again.

The earth grew dense with grain at my desire;
The shade was deepened at the springs and streams;
Moving in dust that clung like pillared fire,
The gathering herds grew heavy in my dreams.

Across the mountains, naked from the heights,
Down to the valley broken settlers came,
And in my houses feasted through the nights,
Rebuilt their sinews and assumed a name.

In my clear rivers my own men discerned
The motive for the ruin and the crime—
Gold heavier than earth, a wealth unearned,
Loot, for two decades, from the heart of Time.

Metal, intrinsic value, deep and dense,
Preanimate, inimitable, still,
Real, but an evil with no human sense,
Dispersed the mind to concentrate the will.

Grained by alchemic change, the human kind
Turned from themselves to rivers and to rocks;
With dynamite broke metal unrefined;
Measured their moods by geologic shocks.

With knives they dug the metal out of stone;
Turned rivers back, for gold through ages piled,
Drove knives to hearts, and faced the gold alone;
Valley and river ruined and reviled;

Reviled and ruined me, my servant slew,
Strangled him from the figtree by my door.
When they had done what fury bade them do,
I was a cursing beggar, stripped and sore.

What end impersonal, what breathless age,
Incontinent of quiet and of years,
What calm catastrophe will yet assuage
This final drouth of penitential tears?

THE CALIFORNIA OAKS

Spreading and low, unwatered, concentrate
Of years of growth that thickens, not expands,
With leaves like mica and with roots that grate
Upon the deep foundations of these lands,
In your brown shadow, on your heavy loam
—Leaves shrinking to the whisper of decay—
What feet have come to roam,
                      what eyes to stay?
Your motion has o'ertaken what calm hands?

Quick as a sunbeam, when a bird divides
The lesser branches, on impassive ground,
Hwui-Shan, the ancient, for a moment glides,
Demure with wisdom, and without a sound;
Brown feet that come to meet him, quick and shy,
Move in the flesh, then, browner, dry to bone;
The brook-like shadows lie
                    where sun had shone;
Ceaseless, the dead leaves gather, mound on mound.

And where they gather, darkening the glade,
In hose and doublet, and with knotty beard,
Armed with the musket and the pirate's blade,
Stern as the silence by the savage feared,
Drake and his seamen pause to view the hills,
Measure the future with a steady gaze.
But when they go naught fills
                    the patient days;
The bay lies empty where the vessels cleared.

The Spaniard, learning caution from the trees,
Building his dwelling from the native clay,
Took native concubines: the blood of these
Calming his blood, he made a longer stay.
Longer, but yet recessive, for the change
Came on his sons and their sons to the end;
For peace may yet derange
                    and earth may bend
The ambitious mind to an archaic way.

Then the invasion! and the soil was turned,
The hidden waters drained, the valleys dried;
And whether fire or purer sunlight burned,
No matter! one by one the old oaks died.
Died or are dying! The archaic race—
Black oak, live oak, and valley oak—ere long
Must crumble on the place
                          which they made strong
And in the calm they guarded now abide.

TO THE MOON

Goddess of poetry,
Maiden of icy stone
With no anatomy,
Between us two alone
Your light falls thin and sure
On all that I propound.

Your service I have found
To be no sinecure;
For I must still inure
My words to what I find,
Though it should leave me blind
Ere I discover how.

What brings me here? Old age.
Here is the written page.
What is your pleasure now?

AT THE SAN FRANCISCO AIRPORT

To my daughter, 1954

This is the terminal: the light
Gives perfect vision, false and hard;
The metal glitters, deep and bright.
Great planes are waiting in the yard—
They are already in the night.

And you are here beside me, small,
Contained and fragile, and intent
On things that I but half recall—
Yet going whither you are bent.
I am the past, and that is all.

But you and I in part are one:
The frightened brain, the nervous will,
The knowledge of what must be done,
The passion to acquire the skill
To face that which you dare not shun.

The rain of matter upon sense
Destroys me momently. The score:
There comes what will come. The expense
Is what one thought, and something more—
One's being and intelligence.

This is the terminal, the break.
Beyond this point, on lines of air,
You take the way that you must take;
And I remain in light and stare—
In light, and nothing else, awake.

Brewster Ghiselin
(1903-   )

LOVE LETTER

Passing and passing
in my grey house
you are always putting to shame
the splendor of the angels.

Don't think of this. . . . Listen:
the ordinary sparrows.

I found it between
a thought and a thought.

Something is growing,
changing alive
under the fallen
leaves of words.

THE CATCH

The track of a broad rattler, dragged over dust at dawn, led us
Across the flats of morning under mesquite and paloverdes,
Path direct as hunger, up to a heaped grace of shade
Rodents had riddled into a hill of galleries. There it ended.

We dug into dust to take alive a lord of venom, whole
Rope and writhe as thick as a child's thigh, in halls of his Hell.

But what we found, under a crust crumpling to knives of spades,
Was a path of fury: earth as light and loose as a harrow beds,
Smell of plowland cut and clawed, and darker down in the mound
A sprawling rag of dragon's pearly armor slubbered with mud.

The feasting grave trembled. It shook us. We heard the darkness grunt.
A snout full of snarls, of a hound or a hog, heaved the spade up and dug
                under.

But was stopped in its tunneling by the steel, as steel was stopped in its teeth.
It turned
Quick, clawing and snapping up light, it charged and a choker rolled it at
pole's end
A badger strap-throttled, flipping like a marlin, battling like a bull on a gaff
And snoring anger till over his bravery and scuffling the door of a cage
clapped.

Burrowing bearclaws rattled in tin. He tasted wire all round.
He bucked, he bruised the ceiling, lunged at a beam and was eating oakwood.

But for that ravening he lived unfed and unslaked. His stench was immense,
His dung was the curved needle ribs of reptiles. He never slept—
Daylong, nightlong. His furious freedom resounded. At starlit dawn
Jaws and claws rasping and thudding thump of his thunder drummed once.
Long

Silences rang for him, cage-eater greedy of snakes, abroad in the dawn.

MARLIN

The wand of that fisherman witching the waves
Dips,
Feeling an abyss,
Lifts
Shuddering, buckling. It has hooked the tide.

Heartstring out of his reel
Screams, the sea
Fountains pieces of itself vomiting its vitals
Far from the boat
Something falling leaping

Skips like a keel—
Is up!
Brandishing, brandishing, a muscle, a rib: an arm,
Like God's
Torn off alive.

Tireless, until—as if the tide itself
Failed or the sea
Changed,
No more averse
Gave up its secret with strange irony

Under shrill-screaming unseemly seabirds' crisscross
Of augury—
Slow as a floating lily, mottled with sea-glyphs, fingered by the waters
Like an island,
Like its own sundown it glides in to die.

VANTAGE

I
All over the blue
Ocean the trees of the whales' breath:
All over the ocean,
Around the steeps of the headland
Falling westward and northward,
Punta Banda, and southward toward the turn of the land,
        three hundred miles,
Toward the lagoons, the pools of calm on the coast of deserts:
The fountains of the breath of the beasts
Whitening and leaning in the wind
On the ocean curve of the world,
Floating and misting,
Into mist
        into distance
               into light.

The time is not yet
Of the continent-cities
And the forests cut.

When our age of glass is no more
Than glitter in dunes
Of detritus
The clouds will be here
In season, the water
Always.

The regret will be gone.

II
Ocean and air will lift
Shoring combers pluming
Over their leaning green
In landwind wings of spume.

If creatures astir on the cliffs
Have then the gift of light, let it
Be larger than ours, that lost
The world and took the moon.

LIGHT

When the poles have gone under the gauzes of our fog and a withering of
                                    icecaps
Is watering our deserts and dikes are rising and land is too little
Despite the high piers fattening into cities and beyond them suburban
Archipelagos of barges broadening our pleasure on all of the earth's
Waters and the moon our quarry is blazing from pockets of her rock
And powdering from her cut mountains and uplifting from the smelters of
                                    her plains
The breath of our life and over her light is curling and curving
The opal of glaucoma our night will long have been blinded of far
More than her brilliance that will have preceded the sun and have followed
Out of heaven the stars we were reading a little as they tarried into exile.

SONG AT SAN CARLOS BAY

Poled high on his cactus over a cliff of desert island, the osprey
Dipping his head at leisure slivers quivering silver, alive
A long while; then settling erect to stillness whitens his breast to the sun.

Slow waves flow in from the open distance and arm of ocean, bright sea of
Cortés,
And over the tiderock under my cliff the white of the ebb rises and spreads
Thinning along the brown of the rock and down to the gathering trough of its
fall.

*

If there are other worlds (there may be—must be—amid the billion trillions,
And more, of the stars) they cannot be wholly as this one is: the torrent of
the galaxy
Falling—as I saw it today before dawn—down the whole height of the dark to
the ocean
Could not be as here, that momentary mist of a cataract so slowly floating it
seems
Unchanged forever, the same after fifty years as I saw it when first its light
Untangled to curve and cluster in constellations, Scorpio, Sagittarius, sea stars
The crickets of a cliff long crumbled landward and blind with houselights
cried under and are quiet.

*

High on his cactus cliff the osprey leaning to unfold
His flight to the wind floats opening the forms of his motion flowing
And rises away to beat the light of his vantage and to fall.

La Montaña Encantada, high westward blunted with cloud, is sharpening its
stone to the sun.

*

As for those other worlds, islands ranging the waste alive
Like ours in the sway of a sun, I see—for analogy is blind to reveal them—
Only how each from our own and all from all of the others may differ,
Vastly in aspect, little in the mode of their ordering, alike as the stars are.

*

19

To the osprey the span of the osprey is sufficient. Even in its moment
Of engendering, the germ of the life of the bird is unfolding wings
And hackling a ninefold hook to hang the blood of the sea
On the thorny air. So I in the instant of embrace that began me
Was opening my arms, to love and death, and my eyes to a vast.

*

Where is the end of space? a child said, to the infinite iterations of the
                                    crickets,
To the tangle of his stars. How is there an end of it? Or how no end? "It is
                                    space
All the way out. . . ." No answer, but abundance—hard horn of dilemma
                                    broken
By absurdity to sweetness, antinomies darkening to restore to us the
                                    enormity of night.

*

If being is the heart of that mystery—as it is of ours, who are in it and of it—
Its truth is not chanted in the noon of the grasshoppers or measured in the
                                    spangle of our stars,
But in silence and darkness: in deliverance from the figure of an image, our
                                    own in presumption,
Familiar of voice or face, or other particular of light to configure it,
Ground and palm and nest of fire, to reveal it in the mode of its ordering. . . .

It could not, I think, be narrow as purpose is—so careless and so careful:
Careless of all but itself, slitting its fish tail-first, though anguish
Quiver with double force, of life and of death-throe, careful and sure
To hold with hooks what is purely its own sweetness and never to relinquish.

*

Evening begins, with a darkening of blue on the sea and a darkening of
                                    shadow on the rockroost,
The island of birds. The sun is yet high, the clouds are the same—hesitations
                                    of wings.
And no bird descends but to feed. The gannets will swing and drop to the
                                    water until dusk.
The spouting foam of the pelicans' fall on the swarming waves will detonate
                                    like depthcharges,
An hour or more, till planets hover the west, and the stars that are veiled with
                                    light,
Canopus over the sea, Sirius, and Rigel of Orion, are hiding the dark.

Earle Birney
(1904-   )

THE BEAR ON THE DELHI ROAD

Unreal   tall as a myth
by the road the Himalayan bear
is beating the brilliant air
with his crooked arms
About him two men   bare
spindly as locusts   leap

One pulls on a ring
in the great soft nose   His mate
flicks   flicks with a stick
up at the rolling eyes

They have not led him here
down from the fabulous hills
to this bald alien plain
and the clamorous world   to kill
but simply to teach him to dance

They are peaceful both   these spare
men of Kashmir   and the bear
alive is their living   too
If   far on the Delhi way
around him galvanic they dance
it is merely to wear   wear
from his shaggy body the tranced
wish forever to stay
only an ambling bear
four-footed in berries

It is no more joyous for them
in this hot dust to prance
out of reach of the praying claws
sharpened to paw for ants
in the shadows of deodars
It is not easy to free
myth from reality
or rear this fellow up
to lurch   lurch with them
in the tranced dancing of men

BIOGRAPHY

At ten the years made tracks
plumped and sprung with pine-needles

Gaining height   overlooked
rock balanced on ridges
swords of snow in cliffside

Twenty he lay by the lake
the bright unpredictable book
gracefully bound in green
and riffled its pages for rainbow

Life was a pup-tent   ptarmigan
chased along simmering slopes
bannocks and bacon
Only the night-mists died at dawn

By thirty he trudged above timber
peered over ice at the peaks

As they swung slowly around him
the veins of bald glaciers blackened
white pulses of waterfalls
beat in the bare rockflesh

Before him at forty
a nunatak stood like a sundial
swiftly marked time in the snow

Later a lancet of rime
hissed from the heave of the massif
a shrill wind shouldered him
and he turned

but tried without might
had lost the lake or his nerve
forgot all the trail-forks
knew at the end only
the ice knuckling his eyes

BUSHED

He invented a rainbow but lightning struck it
shattered it into the lake-lap of a mountain
so big his mind slowed when he looked at it

Yet he built a shack on the shore
learned to roast porcupine belly and
wore the quills on his hatband

At first he was out with the dawn
whether it yellowed bright as wood-columbine
or was only a fuzzed moth in a flannel of storm
But he found the mountain was clearly alive
sent messages whizzing down every hot morning
boomed proclamations at noon and spread out
a white guard of goat
before falling asleep on its feet at sundown

When he tried his eyes on the lake   ospreys
would fall like valkyries
choosing the cut-throat
He took then to waiting
till the night smoke rose from the boil of the sunset

But the moon carved unknown totems
out of the lakeshore
owls in the beardusky woods derided him
moosehorned cedars circled his swamps and tossed
their antlers up to the stars
then he knew   though the mountain slept   the winds
were shaping its peak to an arrowhead
poised

And now he could only
bar himself in and wait
for the great flint to come singing into his heart

EL GRECO: *ESPOLIO*

The carpenter is intent on the pressure of his hand

on the awl   and the trick of pinpointing his strength
through the awl to the wood   which is tough
He has no effort to spare for despoilings
or to worry if he'll be cut in on the dice
His skill is vital to the scene   and the safety of the state
Anyone can perform the indignities   It's his hard arms
and craft that hold the eyes of the convict's women
There is the problem of getting the holes exact
(in the middle of this elbowing crowd)
and deep enough to hold the spikes
after they've sunk through those bared feet
and inadequate wrists he knows are waiting behind him

He doesn't sense perhaps that one of the hands
is held in a curious gesture over him —
giving   or asking   forgiveness? —
but he'd scarcely take time to be puzzled by poses
Criminals come in all sorts
as anyone knows who makes crosses
are as mad or sane as those who decide on their killings
Our one at least has been quiet so far
though they say he talked himself into this trouble
a carpenter's son who got notions of preaching

Well here's a carpenter's son who'll have carpenter sons
God willing   and build what's wanted
temples or tables   mangers or crosses
and shape them decently
working alone in that firm and profound abstraction
which blots out the bawling of rag-snatchers
To construct with hands   knee-weight   braced thigh
keeps the back turned from death

But it's too late now for the other carpenter's boy
to return to this peace before the nails are hammered

IRAPUATO

For reasons any
                brigadier
                            could tell
this is a favorite nook for
                                massacre
Toltex by Mixtex Mixtex by Aztex
Aztex by Spanishtex Spanishtex by
Mexitex by Mexitex by Mexitex by Texaco

So any farmer can see how the strawberries
are the biggest and reddest
                in the whole damn continent

but why
        when arranged under
                            the market flies

do they look like small clotting hearts?

LOOKING FROM OREGON

"And what it watches is not our wars" (Robinson Jeffers)

Far out as I can see
into the crazy dance of light
there are cormorants like little black eyebrows
wriggling and drooping
        but the eye is out of all proportion

Nearer   just beyond the roiling surf
salmon   young or the sperm-heavy
are being overtaken by bird's neb
sealion's teeth   fisherman's talon

The spent waters
        flecks in this corner of the eyeball
falling past my friend and his two sons
        where they straddle the groin's head
collapse on the beach
        after the long race
from where? perhaps from Tonkin's gulf
        on the bloodshot edge

There's no good my searching the horizon
        I'm one of those another poet* saw
        sitting beside our other ocean
I can't look farther out or in

Yet up here in the wild parsnips and the wind
I know the earth is not holding
tumbles in body-lengths
towards thunderheads and unimaginable Asia

though below me on the frothy rocks
my friend and his two boys
do not look up from fishing

*Robert Frost: *Neither Out Far Nor In Deep.*

MAN IS A SNOW

Not the cougar leaping to myth
from the orange lynx of our flame
not the timber swooning to death
in the shock of the saw's bright whine
but the rotograved lie
and a nursery of crosses abroad

Not the death of the prairie grass
in the blind wheat's unheeding
but the harvest mildewed in doubt
and the starved in the hour of our hoarding
not the rivers we foul but our blood
o cold and more devious rushing

Man is a snow that cracks
the trees' red resinous arches
and winters the cabined heart
till the chilled nail shrinks in the wall
and pistols the brittle air
till frost like ferns of the world that is lost
unfurls on the darkening window

SONG FOR SUNSETS

goodnite sun
im turning over again
im on the little ball
so slowly rolling
backwards from you

i hope youre there
burning away
central & responsible
all thru the black
of my dumb
somersault

i'll tumble around
& wake to you
the one who never sleeps
never notices
too busy keeping the whole
flock of us
rolling towards vega
without losing
our milky way

goodnite big dad
hasta la vista
hasta luego
we'll switch on now
our own small stars
& lie in darkness burning
turning
thru unspace untime
& upsadaisy back
i trust
to you

THERE ARE DELICACIES

there are delicacies in you
   like the hearts of watches
there are wheels that turn
   on the tips of rubies
& tiny intricate locks

i need your help
   to contrive keys
there is so little time
   even for the finest
     of watches

WAR WINTERS

Sun
proud Bessemer   peltwarmer beauty
these winters yoke us   We scan sky for you
The dun droppings blur   we drown in snow
In this tarnished chimneyplug   in a tenantless room
this sucked wafer   white simpleton
you?

Not
chiefly the months   mould you heartcharmer
to scant hammerdent   on hardiron sky
not alone latitude   to lodgers on this
your slantwhirling lackey   lifecrusted satellite
this your one wrynecked   woedealing
world

WIND-CHIMES IN A TEMPLE RUIN

This is the moment
    for two glass leaves
dangling dumb
    from the temple eaves
This is the instant
    when the sly air breathes
and the tremblers touch
    where no man sees
Who is the moving
    or moved is no matter
but the birth of the possible
    song in the rafter
that dies as the wind goes
    nudging other
broken eaves
    for waiting lovers

Kenneth Rexroth
(1905-   )

THE HANGED MAN

Storm lifts from Wales
And blows dark over England.
And over my head
As I stand above the Teme.
And look out across Ludlow and the dark castle,
And the ringing church tower
Clear bells on the storm
And grey rain on the river,
And me where I will not come again.
And pain I doubt that formal poet ever knew
Who wrote "This is me"
Anent the page of one too cowardly to love.
Ache and hunger fill the lives
Of those who dare not give or take.
Misery is all the lot of the unlovable ones,
And of rejected lovers,
But not one of these knows the empty horror
Of the slow conquering, long fought off,
Realization that love assumed and trusted
Through years of mutual life
Had never been there at all.
The bells of St. Lawrence
Sprinkle their music over the town.
Silver drops, gathered in Bermuda,
Shimmer and are lost in the brown English water.
It is all just like the poet said.

CONFUSION

for Nancy Shores

I pass your home in a slow vermilion dawn,
The blinds are drawn, and the windows are open.
The soft breeze from the lake
Is like your breath upon my cheek.
All day long I walk in the intermittent rainfall.
I pick a vermilion tulip in the deserted park,
Bright raindrops cling to its petals.
At five o'clock it is a lonely color in the city.
I pass your home in a rainy evening,
I can see you faintly, moving between lighted walls.
Late at night I sit before a white sheet of paper,
Until a fallen vermilion petal quivers before me.

FURTHER ADVANTAGES
OF LEARNING

One day in the Library,
Puzzled and distracted,
Leafing through a dull book
I came on a picture
Of the vase containing
Buddha's relics. A chill
Passed over me. I was
Haunted by the touch of
A calm I cannot know,
The opening into that
Busy place of a better world.

THE MIRROR IN THE WOODS

A mirror hung on the broken
Walls of an old summer house
Deep in the dark woods. Nothing
Ever moved in it but the
Undersea shadows of ferns,
Rhododendrons and redwoods.
Moss covered the frame. One day
The gold and glue gave way and
The mirror slipped to the floor.
For many more years it stood
On the shattered boards. Once in
A long time a wood rat would
Pass it by without ever
Looking in. At last we came,
Breaking the sagging door and
Letting in a narrow wedge
Of sunlight. We took the mirror
Away and hung it in my
Daughter's room with a barre before
It. Now it reflects ronds, escartes,
Relevés and arabesques.
In the old house the shadows,
The wood rats and moss work unseen.

YIN AND YANG

It is spring once more in the Coast Range
Warm, perfumed, under the Easter moon.
The flowers are back in their places.
The birds back in their usual trees.
The winter stars set in the ocean.
The summer stars rise from the mountains.
The air is filled with atoms of quicksilver.
Resurrection envelops the earth.
Geometrical, blazing, deathless,
Animals and men march through heaven,
Pacing their secret ceremony.
The Lion gives the moon to the Virgin.
She stands at the crossroads of heaven,

Holding the full moon in her right hand,
A glittering wheat ear in her left.
The climax of the rite of rebirth
Has ascended from the underworld
As proclaimed in light from the zenith.
In the underworld the sun swims
Between the fish called Yes and No.

THE PLACE

for Yvor Winters

Unique planets break
the passing light
the serrate west the rose
graph oscillate and climbing
spark Antares needle and omen
germinate the apical blue
final crystals and absorbent
the thought
extends
secrets bloom
the bell wethers entangled in the waxen brush
the herd climbs out of dust
water speaks
cautious glockenspiel enshroud
nighthawk and bat
the grey herd bubbles
over the edge of the bench
meanders in the jackpine shadows
the Basquo's face spurts light
lambs stumble to calling ewes
the Basquo chews
speaks of Santander
of Yakima in winter
all night sheep speak intermittently
close at dawn
Utter bounty
after voluntary limit
cautiously anticipating
the single cosine
unambitious ballistics

minute focus
asymtotic object
before the fracture of the unsuspected calyx
or star
or haline signature
or the pinion that bloomed in the eclipse
unrequested
or crocus beneath oak leaf
Fabrics diadems spangles
the noetic flesh
the ivory minoan diver
this curve
this tensile promise
fusile apostle
lucent somatic crystal
beneath purple hemlock
the law of freedom
cloth of gold
lily and lotus
Hermetic invisible
eyes pause between invisible
pillars suspend above the white
table

> And as they went on their journey they
> came toward evening to the river Tigris,
> and they lodged there. And when the
> young man went down to wash himself, a
> fish leaped from the water and would have
> devoured him. Then the angel Raphael
> said unto him. Take the fish. And the
> young man laid hold of the fish and cast it
> upon the land.

the lamp
or eye
Even the trough
even the closing scissors
where the northern boar
bled in the broken wall
the helmets turned slowly green
amongst the flat stones
The further room

34

the root of light
the staff
given in the asian night
carried across Europe
planted in Glastonbury
the unguent
broken on the hair
Bread figs cheese olives grapes wine
the swords rest
mustered for war on the field of law
glories of kingdom
o lord of herds
and these
objects
the plume of mimosa
brushing the roof

THE NEW YEAR

for Helen

I walk on the cold mountain above the city
Through the black eucalyptus plantation.
Only a few of the million lights
Penetrate the leaves and the dripping fog.
I remember the wintry stars
In the bare branches of the maples,
In the branches of the chestnuts that are gone.

VALUE NEUTER

Traders, parsons, and stoolpigeons,
Always confuse value and price.
The long epistemological
Debauch of modern philosophy—
The police-professors mull over
Pilate's question. Judas consults
The best income tax attorneys.

DISCRIMINATION

I don't mind the human race.
I've got pretty used to them
In these past twenty-five years.
I don't mind if they sit next
To me on streetcars, or eat
In the same restaurants, if
It's not at the same table.
However, I don't approve
Of a woman I respect
Dancing with one of them. I've
Tried asking them to my home
Without success. I shouldn't
Care to see my own sister
Marry one. Even if she
Loved him, think of the children.
Their art is interesting.
But certainly barbarous.
I'm sure, if given a chance
They'd kill us all in our beds.
And you must admit, they smell.

GROWING

Who are you? Who am I? Haunted
By the dead, by the dead and the past and the
Falling inertia of unreal, dead
Men and things. Haunted by the threat
Of the impersonal, that which
Never will admit the person,
The closed world of things. Who are
You? Coming up out of the
Mineral earth, one pale leaf
Unlike any other unfolding,
And then another, strange, new,
Utterly different, nothing
I ever expected, growing

Up out of my warm heart's blood.
All new, all strange, all different.
Your own leaf pattern, your own
Flower and fruit, but fed from
One root, the root of our fused flesh.
I and thou, from the one to
The dual, from the dual
To the other, the wonderful,
Unending, unfathomable
Process of becoming each
Our selves for each other.

CODICIL

Most of the world's poetry
Is artifice, construction.
No one reads it but scholars.
After a generation
It has grown so overcooked,
It cannot be digested.
There is little I haven't
Read, and dreary stuff it was.
Lamartine—Gower—Tasso—
Or the metaphysicals
Of Cambridge, ancient or modern,
And their American apes.
Of course for years the ruling
Class of English poetry
Has held that that is just what
Poetry is, impersonal
Construction, where personal
Pronouns are never permitted.
If rigorously enough
Applied, such a theory
Produces in practice its
Opposite. The poetry
Of Eliot and Valéry,
Like that of Pope, isn't just

Personal, it is intense,
Subjective revery as
Intimate and revealing,
Embarrassing if you will,
As the indiscretions of
The psychoanalyst's couch.
There is always sufficient
Reason for a horror of
The use of the pronoun, "I."

Theodore Roethke
(1908-1963)

A WALK IN LATE SUMMER

I

A gull rides on the ripples of a dream,
White upon white, slow-settling on a stone;
Across my lawn the soft-backed creatures come;
In the weak light they wander, each alone.
Bring me the meek, for I would know their ways;
I am a connoisseur of midnight eyes.
The small! The small! I hear them singing clear
On the long banks, in the soft summer air.

II

What is there for the soul to understand?
The slack face of the dismal pure inane?
The wind dies down; my will dies with the wind,
God's in that stone, or I am not a man!
Body and soul transcend appearances
Before the caving-in of all that is;
I'm dying piecemeal, fervent in decay;
My moments linger—that's eternity.

III

A late rose ravages the casual eye,
A blaze of being on a central stem.
It lies upon us to undo the lie
Of living merely in the realm of time.
Existence moves toward a certain end—
A thing all earthly lovers understand.
That dove's elaborate way of coming near
Reminds me I am dying with the year.

IV

A tree arises on a central plain—
It is no trick of change or chance of light.
A tree all out of shape from wind and rain,
A tree thinned by the wind obscures my sight.
The long day dies; I walked the woods alone;
Beyond the ridge two wood thrush sing as one.
Being delights in being, and in time.
The evening wraps me, steady as a flame.

SNAKE

I saw a young snake glide
Out of the mottled shade
And hang, limp on a stone:
A thin mouth, and a tongue
Stayed, in the still air.

It turned; it drew away;
Its shadow bent in half;
It quickened, and was gone.

I felt my slow blood warm.
I longed to be that thing,
The pure, sensuous form.

And I may be, some time.

FOURTH MEDITATION

I

I was always one for being alone,
Seeking in my own way, eternal purpose;
At the edge of the field waiting for the pure moment;
Standing, silent, on sandy beaches or walking along green embankments;
Knowing the sinuousness of small waters:
As a chip or shell, floating lazily with a slow current,
A drop of the night rain still in me,
A bit of water caught in a wrinkled crevice,
A pool riding and shining with the river,
Dipping up and down in the ripples,
Tilting back the sunlight.

Was it yesterday I stretched out the thin bones of my innocence?
O the songs we hide, singing only to ourselves!

Once I could touch my shadow, and be happy;
In the white kingdoms, I was light as a seed,
Drifting with the blossoms,
A pensive petal.

But a time comes when the vague life of the mouth no longer suffices;
The dead make more impossible demands from their silence;
The soul stands, lonely in its choice,
Waiting, itself a slow thing,
In the changing body.

    The river moves, wrinkled by midges,
    A light wind stirs in the pine needles.
    The shape of a lark rises from a stone;
    But there is no song.

II
What is it to be a woman?
To be contained, to be a vessel?
To prefer a window to a door?
A pool to a river?
To become lost in a love,
Yet remain only half aware of the intransient glory?
To be a mouth, a meal of meat?
To gaze at a face with the fixed eyes of a spaniel?

I think of the self-involved:
The ritualists of the mirror, the lonely drinkers,
The minions of benzedrine and paraldehyde,
And those who submerge themselves deliberately in trivia,
Women who become their possessions,
Shapes stiffening into metal,
Match-makers, arrangers of picnics—
What do their lives mean,
And the lives of their children?—

The young, brow-beaten early into a baleful silence,
Frozen by a father's lip, a mother's failure to answer.
Have they seen, ever, the sharp bones of the poor?
Or known, once, the soul's authentic hunger,
Those cat-like immaculate creatures
For whom the world works?

What do they need?
O more than a roaring boy,
For the sleek captains of intuition cannot reach them;
They feel neither the tearing iron
Nor the sound of another footstep—
How I wish them awake!
May the high flower of the hay climb into their hearts;
May they lean into light and live;
May they sleep in robes of green, among the ancient ferns;
May their eyes gleam with the first dawn;
May the sun gild them a worm;
May they be taken by the true burning;
May they flame into being!—

I see them as figures walking in a greeny garden,
Their gait formal and elaborate, their hair a glory,
The gentle and beautiful still-to-be-born;
The descendants of the playful tree-shrew that survived the archaic killers,
The fang and the claw, the club and the knout, the irrational edict,
The fury of the hate-driven zealot, the meanness of the human weasel;
Who turned a corner in time, when at last he grew a thumb;
A prince of small beginnings, enduring the slow stretches of change,
Who spoke first in the coarse short-hand of the subliminal depths,
Made from his terror and dismay a grave philosophical language;
A lion of flame, pressed to the point of love,
Yet moves gently among the birds.

III

Younglings, the small fish keep heading into the current.
What's become of care? This lake breathes like a rose.
Beguile me, change. What have I fallen from?
I drink my tears in a place where all light comes.
I'm in love with the dead! My whole forehead's a noise!
On a dark day I walk straight toward the rain.
Who else sweats light from a stone?
By singing we defend;
The husk lives on, ardent as a seed;
My back creaks with the dawn.

Is my body speaking? I breathe what I am:
The first and last of all things.
Near the graves of the great dead,
Even the stones speak.

MEDITATION AT OYSTER RIVER

I

Over the low, barnacled, elephant-colored rocks,
Come the first tide-ripples, moving, almost without sound, toward me
Running along the narrow furrows of the shore, the rows of dead clam shells;
Then a runnel behind me, creeping closer,
Alive with tiny striped fish, and young crabs climbing in and out of the
         water.

No sound from the bay. No violence.
Even the gulls quiet on the far rocks,
Silent, in the deepening light,
Their cat-mewing over,
Their child-whimpering.

At last one long undulant ripple,
Blue-black from where I am sitting,
Makes almost a wave over a barrier of small stones,
Slapping lightly against a sunken log.
I dabble my toes in the brackish foam sliding forward,
Then retire to a rock higher up on the cliff-side.
The wind slackens, light as a moth fanning a stone:

A twilight wind, light as a child's breath
Turning not a leaf, not a ripple.
The dew revives on the beach-grass;
The salt-soaked wood of a fire crackles;
A fish raven turns on its perch (a dead tree in the rivermouth),
Its wings catching a last glint of the reflected sunlight.

II
The self persists like a dying star,
In sleep, afraid. Death's face rises afresh,
Among the shy beasts, the deer at the salt-lick,
The doe with its sloped shoulders loping across the highway,
The young snake, poised in green leaves, waiting for its fly,
The hummingbird, whirring from quince-blossom to morning-glory—
With these I would be.

And with water: the waves coming forward, without cessation,
The waves, altered by sand-bars, beds of kelp, miscellaneous driftwood,
Topped by cross-winds, tugged at by sinuous undercurrents
The tide rustling in, sliding between the ridges of stone,
The tongues of water, creeping in, quietly.

III
In this hour,
In this first heaven of knowing,
The flesh takes on the pure poise of the spirit,
Acquires, for a time, the sandpiper's insouciance,
The hummingbird's surety, the kingfisher's cunning—
I shift on my rock, and I think:
Of the first trembling of a Michigan brook in April,
Over a lip of stone, the tiny rivulet;
And that wrist-thick cascade tumbling from a cleft rock,
Its spray holding a double rain-bow in early morning,
Small enough to be taken in, embraced, by two arms,—
Or the Tittebawasee, in the time between winter and spring,
When the ice melts along the edges in early afternoon.
And the midchannel begins cracking and heaving from the pressure beneath,
The ice piling high against the iron-bound spiles,
Gleaming, freezing hard again, creaking at midnight—
And I long for the blast of dynamite,

The sudden sucking roar as the culvert loosens its debris of branches and
     sticks,
Welter of tin cans, pails, old bird nests, a child's shoe riding a log,
As the piled ice breaks away from the battered spiles,
And the whole river begins to move forward, its bridges shaking.

IV
Now, in this waning of light,
I rock with the motion of morning;
In the cradle of all that is,
I'm lulled into half-sleep
By the lapping of water,
Cries of the sandpiper.
Water's my will, and my way,
And the spirit runs, intermittently,
In and out of the small waves,
Runs with the intrepid shorebirds—
How graceful the small before danger!

In the first of the moon,
All's a scattering,
A shining.

HER TIME

When all
My waterfall
Fancies sway away
From me, in the sea's silence;
In the time
When the tide moves
Neither forward nor back,
And the small waves
Begin rising whitely,
And the quick winds
Flick over the close whitecaps,
And two scoters fly low,
Their four wings beating together,
And my salt-laden hair
Flies away from my face
Before the almost invisible
Spray, and the small shapes
Of light on the far
Cliff disappear in a last
Glint of the sun, before
The long surf of the storm booms
Down on the near shore,
When everything—birds, men, dogs—
Runs to cover:
I'm one to follow,
To follow.

ELEGY

Her face like a rain-beaten stone on the day she rolled off
With the dark hearse, and enough flowers for an alderman,—
And so she was, in her way, Aunt Tilly.

Sighs, sighs, who says they have sequence?
Between the spirit and the flesh,—what war?
She never knew;

For she asked no quarter and gave none,
Who sat with the dead when the relatives left,
Who fed and tended the infirm, the mad, the epileptic,
And, with a harsh rasp of a laugh at herself,
Faced up to the worst.

I recall how she harried the children away all the late summer
From the one beautiful thing in her yard, the peachtree;
How she kept the wizened, the fallen, the misshapen for herself
And picked and pickled the Best, to be left on rickety doorsteps.

And yet she died in agony,
Her tongue, at the last, thick, black as an ox's.

Terror of cops, bill collectors, betrayers of the poor,—
I see you in some celestial supermarket,
Moving serenely among the leeks and cabbages,
Probing the squash,
Bearing down, with two steady eyes,
On the quaking butcher.

THE MEADOW MOUSE

I

In a shoe box stuffed in an old nylon stocking
Sleeps the baby mouse I found in the meadow,
Where he trembled and shook beneath a stick
Till I caught him up by the tail and brought him in,
Cradled in my hand,
A little quaker, the whole body of him trembling,
His absurd whiskers sticking out like a cartoon-mouse,
His feet like small leaves,
Little lizard-feet,
Whitish and spread wide when he tried to struggle away,
Wriggling like a miniscule puppy.

Now he's eaten his three kinds of cheese and drunk from his bottle-cap
    watering-trough—
So much he just lies in one corner,
His tail curled under him, his belly big
As his head; his bat-like ears
Twitching, tilting toward the least sound.
Do I imagine he no longer trembles
When I come close to him?
He seems no longer to tremble.

II
But this morning the shoe-box house on the back porch is empty.
Where has he gone, my meadow mouse,
My thumb of a child that nuzzled in my palm?—
To run under the hawk's wing,
Under the eye of the great owl watching from the elm-tree,
To live by courtesy of the shrike, the snake, the tom-cat.

I think of the nestling fallen into the deep grass,
The turtle gasping in the dusty rubble of the highway,
The paralytic stunned in the tub, and the water rising,—
All things innocent, hapless, forsaken.

IN A DARK TIME

In a dark time, the eye begins to see,
I meet my shadow in the deepening shade;
I hear my echo in the echoing wood—
A lord of nature weeping to a tree.
I live between the heron and the wren,
Beasts of the hill and serpents of the den.

What's madness but nobility of soul
At odds with circumstance? The day's on fire!
I know the purity of pure despair,
My shadow pinned against a sweating wall.
That place among the rocks—is it a cave,
Or winding path? The edge is what I have.

A steady storm of correspondences!
A night flowing with birds, a ragged moon,
And in broad day the midnight come again!
A man goes far to find out what he is—
Death of the self in a long, tearless night,
All natural shapes blazing unnatural light.

Dark, dark my light and darker my desire.
My soul, like some heat-maddened summer fly,
Keeps buzzing at the sill. Which I is *I*?
A fallen man, I climb out of my fear.
The mind enters itself, and God the mind,
And one *is* One, free in the tearing wind.

IN EVENING AIR

I
A dark theme keeps me here,
Though summer blazes in the vireo's eye.
Who would be half possessed
By his own nakedness?
Waking's my care—
I'll make a broken music, or I'll die.

II
Ye littles, lie more close!
Make me, O Lord, a last, a simple thing
Time cannot overwhelm.
Once I transcended time:
A bud broke to a rose,
And I rose from a last diminishing.

III
I look down the far light
And I behold the dark side of a tree
Far down a billowing plain,
And when I look again,
It's lost upon the night—
Night I embrace, a dear proximity.

IV
I stand by a low fire
Counting the wisps of flame, and I watch how
Light shifts upon the wall.
I bid stillness be still.
I see, in evening air,
How slowly dark comes down on what we do.

THE SEQUEL

I
Was I too glib about eternal things,
An intimate of air and all its songs?
Pure aimlessness pursued and yet pursued
And all wild longings of the insatiate blood
Brought me down to my knees. O who can be
Both moth and flame? The weak moth blundering by.
Whom do we love? I thought I knew the truth;
Of grief I died, but no one knew my death.

II
I saw a body dancing in the wind,
A shape called up out of my natural mind;
I heard a bird stir in its true confine;
A nestling sighed—I called that nestling mine;
A partridge drummed; a minnow nudged its stone;
We danced, we danced, under a dancing moon;
And on the coming of the outrageous dawn,
We danced together, we danced on and on.

III
Morning's a motion in a happy mind:
She stayed in light, as leaves live in the wind,
Swaying in air, like some long water weed.
She left my body, lighter than a seed;
I gave her body full and grave farewell.
A wind came close, like a shy animal.
A light leaf on a tree, she swayed away
To the dark beginnings of another day.

THE MOTION

I

The soul has many motions, body one.
An old wind-tattered butterfly flew down
And pulsed its wings upon the dusty ground—
Such stretchings of the spirit make no sound.
By lust alone we keep the mind alive,
And grieve into the certainty of love.

II

Love begets love. This torment is my joy.
I watch a river wind itself away;
To meet the world, I rise up in my mind;
I hear a cry and lose it on the wind.
What we put down, must we take up again?
I dare embrace. By striding, I remain.

III

Who but the loved know love's a faring-forth?
Who's old enough to live?—a thing of earth
Knowing how all things alter in the seed
Until they reach this final certitude,
This reach beyond this death, this act of love
In which all creatures share, and thereby live,

IV

Wings without feathers creaking in the sun,
The close dirt dancing on a sunless stone
God's night and day: down this space He has smiled,
Hope has its hush: we move through its broad day,—
O who would take the vision from the child?
O, motion O, our chance is still to be!

THE DECISION

I

What shakes the eye but the invisible?
Running from God's the longest race of all.
A bird kept haunting me when I was young—
The phoebe's slow retreating from its song,
Nor could I put that sound out of my mind,
The sleepy sound of leaves in a light wind.

II

Rising or falling's all one discipline!
The line of my horizon's growing thin!
Which is the way? I cry to the dread black,
The shifting shade, the cinders at my back.
Which is the way? I ask, and turn to go,
As a man turns to face on-coming snow.

Veneta Nielsen
(1909-   )

FAMILIAR

"Comes a sparrow and quickly through that house flies. Comes through one door in and through another door out departs."—*Bede*

Her eyes began to darken when she said she saw it,
Really, the black bird flew straight at her
Out of the middle of her television screen.
She tried to catch, then drive it doorwards, crowding,
Only it swooped around, and round and round,
In noisy silence, fluttered, battered,
Kept above her reach then vanished utterly,
Into the air exactly in the way a black bird vanished
More than sixty years ago before her mother's eyes
Although her mother chased him with a broom.

    Neighbor and friend of blue eyes now grown dark
    As smoke buds whispered, offering shyly
    To hide a dead bird underneath a sofa, out of sight . . .
    As if my mother could be fooled. . . . Her neighbor meant well
    And to mean well is to love.

This morning in three-shadowed sunlight Mother's eyes
Where black-brown wells too deep to look back into
As she pointed to her tree, the faithful apple
She helped my father plant so long ago; since then
The tree who should have had a name poured apples
In red drifts toward her providence of shelf.
Something has taken her, the withered apples
Shrink in green felty wrinkles, and the leaves
Are mottling strangely, some are leaden gray and dry
As if the future isn't going to have a need.

Now in my mind's eye stands my absent youthful father,
On school house steps, striking a bright triangle—
Mind's ear hears the hum, the vibrant tingle-tangle,
That brought his silent noisy pupils, after recess,
Quickly back into his room.

I say her vision must be watched, new lenses ordered,
Her picture tube renewed, antennae checked.
I'll get a horticulture expert for dear Apple,
Consult the books on telesthetic birds. . . .
She searches her long album. All my theory stops
Somewhere between teloptic wings and tree.
His schoolroom clatters with assembled voices.
There goes his pitchpipe, some begin to sing.
Geometry's my hardest subject. What's an image
Of a space that has dimension without time?

Jerky and wordless, like a flickershow
Her channels jumble April and December.
My mother thinks, is trying to remember
Some sequence reconciling "I Love Lucy," with
How quietly comes the snow.

Clarice Short
(1910-   )

WINTERKILL

The winterkill
Can hurt the heart too deeply for the spring
To heal or cheer.
There is no solace in the greening hill
Where thin blades of the dogtooth violets stab
Through the white rib cage of the deer.

ON THE SHORE OF CRETE

It would not be unfitting
To die here on the shore of Crete
Between mountains that look like my own
And the sea whose rhythmic run up the smooth beach
Sounds like the calm breathing of a large beast.

I have prepared as well as I could:
Walked through fields of blossoming asphodel,
Saved the right coin for the fare of passage,
Laid by small stores of bread and wine.

But there is the problem of disposal:
International regulations are involved;
One may not simply be covered with a little earth
So as not to become food for scavengers.
I have envied the sodden gull that for a while
Is decently covered with feathers until the whole
Is swept away by a wave to the great deep
Or assimilated by the patient sand.

WORK OF ART

The great trout shone
Silver, deep down in stream so airy clear
The yellow leaves the current bore along
Made perfect silhouettes on him as they passed
And on the slab of slate on which he lay.

In language only half decipherable,
Total frustration spoke in baffling beauty:
The trout, long master of that circling pool
At the fall's edge, had taken the grey gnat
At twilight, as before, but on the bank
Some fisherman had seen the swirl and felt
The line strain, the pole bend, and knew the prey
No naive summerling, but in the dusk
Caught only glimpses of a flashing form
That once arched through the surface like bright blade.

Then in the current the line floated free.
Known bonds were broken, but mysteriously
The pool held fast its own; invisible barbs
Held the trout fettered to the seams of slate.
In icy water perfectly preserved,
He lay, a silver image fused on lead,
Under crystal flecked with gold.

THE WHETSTONE

"Let me put an edge on that hoe,"
My father would say, drawing from his pocket
The whetstone that he carried to the field.
(He knew perhaps that the rows were getting long,
And the weeds in the corn putting up more resistance.)

Or, as we skinned the squirrels, "Let me see that knife."
(The skin of a squirrel being put on him to stay.)
And with a few deft strokes along the blade
Make edges no integument could withstand
And set us going again with hope renewed.

56

The grindstone in the shop did the heavier work,
And I have turned as told while axe or scythe
He held so that the stone bit where it should
To leave a perfect bezel on the blade
That sloped in gentle luster out of sight.

He could have left me lesser legacies
Than a fine whetstone and a lively sense
Of responsibility for the cutting edge.

ENCOUNTER

From the tracks it appeared
That one stood in the snow and looked at the one who lay
Face down in the snow. The yearling that wandered away
From the herd in the draw had neared
The quiet object silvered over with frost
And then returned softly over the way he came.
There was no exchange between the wild and the tame:
It would even be wrong to say that their paths crossed:
But undoubtedly one was young and the other old.
It may be conjectured that under the star-shot skies
The young looked at the old with uncomprehending eyes,
In the stillness, in the cold.

THE OLD ONE AND THE WIND

She loves the wind.
There on the edge of the known world, at ninety,
In her tall house, any wildness in the elements
Is as welcome as an old friend.
When the surgically patched elms and sycamores
Crack off their heavy limbs in the freak snow storm
Of October, she rejoices; the massy hail
That drives craters into her groomed lawn
Stirs her sluggish heart to a riot of beating.

A cluster of cottonwood trees in the swale
Of the prairie, oasis now in a desert of wheat fields,
Is all that is left of the home place. No one
Is left to remember the days there with her:
The playhouse sheltered behind the cowshed,
The whirlwinds that made a column of corn shucks,
Winters when snow brushed out all the fences,
Springs when the white of the snow turned to daisies,
Wind-bent as were the urchins who picked them.

To her in her tall house in the tame town, the wind
That escapes the windbreaks of man's constructing
Blows from a distance beyond the young's conceiving,
Is rife with excitements of the world's beginning
And its end.

J. V. Cunningham
(1910-   )

THE PHOENIX

More than the ash stays you from nothingness!
Nor here nor there is a consuming pyre!
Your essence is in infinite regress
That burns with varying consistent fire,
Mythical bird that bears in burying!

I have not found you in exhausted breath
That carves its image on the Northern air,
I have not found you on the glass of death
Though I am told that I shall find you there,
Imperturbable in the final cold,

There where the North wind shapes white cenotaphs,
There where snowdrifts cover the fathers' mound,
Unmarked but for these wintry epitaphs,
Still are you singing there without sound,
Your mute voice on the crystal embers flinging.

CONSOLATION NOVA
For Alan Swallow

To speak of death is to deny it, is
To give unpredicated substance phrase
And being. So the discontinuous,
The present instant absent finally
Without future or past, is yet in time
For we are time, monads of purposes
Beyond ourselves that are not purposes,
A causeless all of momentary somes.
And in such fiction we can think of death.

Josephine Miles
(1911-   )

I TELEPHONED A FRIEND . . .

When I telephoned a friend, her husband told me
    She's not here tonight, she's out saving the Bay.
    She is sitting and listening in committee chambers,
    Maybe speaking, with her light voice
    From the fourteenth row, about where
    The birds and fish will go if we fill in the Bay.

    The fish, she says, include starry flounder,
    Pacific herring, rockfish, surfperches,
    And the flat fish who come to the spawning flats
    In the shallow waters near the narrow shores.
    The shadow-look you know, the fish shooting
    In that light green shallow, a dark arrow.

    Otherwise we will get a bowling alley,
    A car park and golf course, with financing,
    Sift up the shallows into a solid base
    With sand dredged from the deeper channels, brought in scows
    Or hopper dredges, and dumped on the fish, and then paved over
    For recreation with no cost to the city.

    And so we hear the sides, the margins speaking:
    To allow the Commission in the public interest
    Permits for the recovery of sand and gravel
    From the submerged tidelands of the State,
    Fill of unlimited quality, clean sand
    Replenished by the southern littoral drift;

    Or yet, Dear Sirs: Your bill flies in the face
    Of the U. S. Army Engineers' Barrier Study,
    The Delta Study, Transportation Study,
    Even the Petroleum Institute plan for bringing freighters
    And hundreds of workers in to Contra Costa
    To boat, bathe, drink, and return these waters.

A student I remember said to me, My mother
Wants me to be a banker, but I want to be
A sanitary engineer, spending all that money
Back toward the sea. Do you think it's possible?
See how these hills shape down back of the college
In summer streaked with little dry arroyos
In winter running over, rush and freshet,
Through storm drains, cellars, sometimes parlors, straight away
Down to the sea. Think of the veins
Of this earth all flowing raining water,
The drove of rivers in the pipes we've laid.
Effluent, said my student, there's a word.
Give me a choice between it and *débris*
And any day I'd choose *effluent.*
Cover and fill is bleach and burn, with tires
Sticking up out of the muck, and loads
Of old brush and tree branches crisping away there.
Nor for me, I like the purest water
Sparkling green under a soil, and it can breeze
Out of our pipes and chemicals, lucent as
The rain itself, around the bodies
Of fish and swimmers.

Saving the bay,
Saving the shoals of day,
Saving the tides of shallows deep begun
Between the moon and sun.

Saving the sidings of the Santa Fé.
Saving the egret and the herring run,
Cane and acacia, mallow and yarrow save,
Against the seventh wave,

Boundary and margin, meeting and met,
So that the pure sea will not forget,
Voracious as it is, its foreign kind,
And so the land,

Voracious as it is, will not redeem
Another's diadem.
Saving the shores,
Saving the lines between

Kelp, shrimp, and the scrub green,
Between the lap of waters
And the long
Shoulder of stone.

Therein, between, no homogeneous dredge,
But seedy edge
Of action and of chance
Met to its multiple and variable circumstance.

Though a news column says that Aquatic Park is a police headache,
In the past year, eighty-seven arrests
Of characters for crimes better not talked about,
That the lake is a favorite dumping spot for hot safes,
Burglary tools, stripped bikes, even a body,

Yet a notice says, Next week at Aquatic Park,
The V-Drive Boating Club holds its annual race—
Everybody comes out for this event—
These are the world's fastest boats faster than hydros,
Needing the quiet water the embankment provides.

And a letter from a statistician, fond of the facts,
Compares the use of Aquatic Park to the Rose Garden: the same pattern;
Fewest people, about five each, on a Friday of terrible weather,
Next, about fifty, on a warm Wednesday afternoon,
Most, a hundred and fifty, on a clear windy Saturday.
        Signed, sincerely, Statistician.

Some live in the deeps, a freighter
Plying between here and Yokohama.
Some live in the rose gardens,
Deeps of a street, a two-storied
Observer and participant, daily
Moving out into the traffic, back into it
Where curtains billow in their breakfast room.
The deeps. Some
Live in the margins. Have they the golden mean?

Freight whistles reach here and the fire engines
Coming from town, foundry hammers
Among the wash of waves.
Kelp drifts them up afloat, and suddenly
They are in the tinder world of lizards.
Cut ashore they bask and breathe
And then plunge back
Down the long glints that take their weight.
At home. At home. But which?

    Likely a sea captain will live in a margin
    But never wants to, wants a deep molded farm;
    Likely an architect, but mainly weekends.
    On the weekdays, along the Bay margin
    Little happens, small objects
    Breed and forage. Flights come in and vanish.
    Solicitudes entail solicitudes.
    Dredge the channel, reinforce the sea wall
    And we shall have deep calling to deep directly.

She starts to speak, my friend in her light voice,
Of margins: marshes, birds, and embarcaderos.
Truths spread to dry like nets, mended like nets,
Draw in at the edges their corruptions,
To let the moving world of bay and town
Mingle, as they were amphibian again.

Saving the bay. Saving the blasted bay.
That there be margins of the difference,
Scrap heap and mobile, wind ridge and ledge,
Mud and débris. That there be
Shore and sea.

THE MAILMAN IS COMING . . .

The mailman is coming from the next block down,
      Where the sycamores thin out and flowering plums
      Begin. A little boy's mother is terrified as he beats his head
      O n the pavement in anger. She is crying, Softer.

      From the next block down, where flowering plums
      Thin to industrial fog, coconut soap on the cottages,
      A great morning squabble races
      In which the big machines call, Softer.

      One letter from the merchants' association asks:
      How improve status in its concrete forms
      Without demolition? How does the Vogue Cleaners
      Sponge off the spot without fraying the coat?

      One from the emporium of knowledge:
      How can we not corrupt answers with questions
      And clearly enough say to the coasting pavement,
      Keep off the grass?

      One from the hill: What do we do
      When the formulas buckle
      And men beat their heads on the pavement
      In pure anger? write them a letter?

      One third-class ad from the snowfields of the Sierras,
      The mailman's birthplace, he says, comes cool
      Across orchards to the bay to say to his readers, Softer,
      Softer.

APART FROM BRANCHES . . .

Apart from branches in courtyards and small stones,
   The countryside is beyond me.
   I can go along University Avenue from Rochester to Sobrante
   And then the Avenue continues to the Bay.

   Often I think of the dry scope of foothill country,
   Moraga Hill, Andreas, Indian country, where I was born
   And where in the scrub the air tells me
   How to be born again.

   Often I think of the long rollers
   Breaking against the beaches
   All the way down the coast to the border
   On bookish cressets and culverts blue and Mediterranean.

   There I break
   In drops of spray as fine as letters
   Blown high, never to be answered,
   But waking am the shore they break upon.

   Both the dry talkers, those old Indians,
   And the dry trollers, those old pirates,
   Say something, but it's mostly louder talking,
   Gavel rapping, and procedural dismays.

   Still where we are, and where we call and call,
   The long rollers of the sea come in
   As if they lived here. The dry Santa Ana
   Sweeps up the town and takes it for a feast.

   Then Rochester to El Sobrante is a distance
   No longer than my name.

WHEN THE SUN CAME . . .

When the sun came, the rooster expanded to meet it,
    Stood up, stirred his wings,
    Raised his red comb and sentence
    Rendered imperative utterance
    Saying, Awake. Nothing answered.
    He took in a beakful of air; yes, first it was he,
    And engendered a number of hard-shelled cacklers,
    One for each day in the week.
    They grew in their yard, the dust in their feathers,
    Who heard them praise him? An egg.

    In the night, in the barn, the eggs wakened and cried,
    Saying, We have been wakened,
    And cried, saying Father, so named him,
    His feathers and beak from the white and the yolk.
    Father, who newly can ring out the welkin,
    And crow, we will listen to hear.
    As toward him we move, and the wings of our feathers grow bright,
    As we spring from the dust into flame
    He will call us his chickens.
    But that was already their name.

IN THE NEIGHBORHOOD . . .

In the neighborhood of my childhood, a hundred lungers
    Coughed in their tents like coyotes.
    The sand was dry and saged with mesquite.
    Even so, from mountains the dew dropped
    Down on the canvas in the early dark.
    The kerosene puffed away as I fell to sleep.

    In that rich landscape I was deprived,
    Because no negro coughed among the tents, moved
    Outward among the distant orange groves.
    A square shot of Indians walked the coals,
    But so pure the absence of black skin, I thought
    All the sorrows of the world were white.

Later, a stonewall neighbor Harriman's
Krazy Kat neither spoke to us, nor spoke
To any negro neighbor because we had none.
Mexican squatters in the boxes in the dry river
˙ Sent no drift of blackness to our dream.
Black Sambo was our child.

When land gave no relief, across the plains
The white and blistered figures in jalopies
Moved into town, but did not come to college.
And so who were they? Such an array
In sandy paleness needed to be brown.
Minority, myself.

Deprived.
Out of the sunny and the shadowy scenes
Where I look back with wonderment and love,
An oversimple marginal deployment
Of absence,
A relentless letting be.

Karl Shapiro
(1913-   )

CALIFORNIA WINTER

It is winter in California, and outside
Is like the interior of a florist shop:
A chilled and moisture-laden crop
Of pink camellias lines the path; and what
Rare roses for a banquet or a bride,
So multitudinous that they seem a glut!

A line of snails crosses the golf-green lawn
From the rosebushes to the ivy bed;
An arsenic compound is distributed
For them. The gardener will rake up the shells
And leave in a corner of the patio
The little mound of empty snails, like skulls.

By noon the fog is burnt off by the sun
And the world's immensest sky opens a page
For the exercises of a future age;
Now jet planes draw straight lines, parabolas
And x's, which the wind, before they're done
Erases leisurely or pulls to fuzz.

It is winter in the valley of the vine.
The vineyards crucified on stakes suggest
War cemeteries, but the fruit is pressed.
The redwood vats are brimming in the shed,
And on the sidings stand tank cars of wine,
For which bright juice a billion grapes have bled.

And skiers from the snow line driving home
Descend through almond orchards, olive farms,
Fig tree and palm tree—everything that warms
The imagination of the wintertime.
If the walls were older one would think of Rome:
If the land were stonier one would think of Spain.

But this land grows the oldest living things,
Trees that were young when Pharaohs ruled the world,
Trees whose new leaves are only just unfurled.
Beautiful they are not; they oppress the heart
With gigantism and with immortal wings;
And yet one feels the sumptuousness of this dirt.

It is raining in California, a straight rain
Cleaning the heavy oranges on the bough,
Filling the gardens till the gardens flow,
Shining the olives, tiling the gleaming tile,
Waxing the dark camellia leaves more green,
Flooding the daylong valleys like the Nile.

THE ALPHABET

The letters of the Jews as strict as flames
Or little terrible flowers lean
Stubbornly upwards through the perfect ages,
Singing through solid stone the sacred names.
The letters of the Jews are black and clean
And lie in chain-line over Christian pages.
The chosen letters bristle like barbed wire
That hedge the flesh of man,
Twisting and tightening the book that warns.
These words, this burning bush, this flickering pyre
Unsacrifices the bled son of man
Yet plaits his crown of thorns.

Where go the tipsy idols of the Roman
Past synagogues of patient time,
Where go the sisters of the Gothic rose,
Where go the blue eyes of the Polish women
Past the almost natural crime,
Past the still speaking embers of ghettos,
There rise the tinder flowers of the Jews.
The letters of the Jews are dancing knives
That carve the heart of darkness seven ways,
These are the letters that all men refuse
And will refuse until the king arrives
And will refuse until the death of time
And all is rolled back in the book of days.

TORNADO WARNING

It is a beauteous morning but the air turns sick,
The April freshness seems to rot, a curious smell.
Above the wool-pack clouds a rumor stains the sky,
A fallow color deadening atmosphere and mind.
The air gasps horribly for breath, sucking itself
In spasms of sharp pain, light drifts away.
Women walk on grass, a few husbands come home,
Bushes and trees stop dead, children gesticulate,
Radios warn to open windows, tell where to hide.

The pocky cloud mammato-cumulus comes on,
Downward-projecting bosses of brown cloud grow
Lumps on lymphatic sky, blains, tumors, and dugs,
Heavy cloud-boils that writhe in general disease of sky,
While bits of hail clip at the crocuses and clunk
At cars and windowglass.

              We cannot see the mouth,
We cannot see the mammoth's neck hanging from cloud,
Snout open, lumbering down ancient Nebraska
Where dinosaur lay down in deeps of clay and died,
And towering elephant fell and billion buffalo.
We cannot see the horror-movie of the funnel-cloud
Snuffing up cows, crazing the cringing villages,
Exploding homes and barns, bursting the level lakes.

MESSIAS

Alone in the darkling apartment the boy
Was reading poetry when the doorbell rang;
The sound sped to his ear and winged his joy,
The book leaped from his lap on broken wing.

Down the gilt stairwell then he peered
Where an old man of patriarchal race
Climbed in an eastern language with his beard
A black halo around his paper face.

His glasses spun with vision and his hat
Was thick with fur in the August afternoon;
His silk suit crackled heavily with light
And in his hand a rattling canister shone.

Bigger he grew and softer the root words
Of the hieratic language of his heart,
And faced the boy, who flung the entrance wide
And fled in terror from the nameless hurt.

Past every door like a dead thing he swam,
Past the entablatures of the kitchen walls,
Down the red ringing of the fire escape
Singing with sun, to the green grass he came,

Sickeningly green, leaving the man to lurch
Bewildered through the house and seat himself
In the sacrificial kitchen after his march,
To study the strange boxes on the shelf.

There mother found him mountainous and alone,
Mumbling some singsong in a monotone,
Crumbling breadcrumbs in his scholar's hand
That wanted a donation for the Holy Land.

TEASING THE NUNS

Up in the elevator went the nuns
    Wild as a cage of undomestic ducks,
Turning and twittering their unclipped hats,
    Gay in captivity, a flirtatious flock
Of waterfowl tipped with black
    Above the traffic and its searing suns.
Higher and higher in the wall we flew
    Hauled on by rosaries and split strands of hair,
Myself in the center sailing like Sinbad
    Yanked into heaven by a hairy Roc;
Whence we emerged into a towery cell
    Where holy cross was splayed upon the wall
In taxidermy of the eternal. They
    Bedecked in elegant bird-names dropped
Curtsies, I thought, and merrily sat
    And fixed their gaze on mine that floated out
Between them and their poised hawk.

"Sisters," I said.—And then I stopped.

THE FIGUREHEAD

Watching my paralytic friend
Caught in the giant clam of himself
Fast on the treacherous shoals of his bed,
I look away to the place he had left
Where at a decade's distance he appeared
To pause in his walk and think of a limp.
One day he arrived at the street bearing
The news that he dragged an ancient foot:
The people on their porches seemed to sway.

Though there are many wired together
In this world and the next, my friend
Strains in his clamps. He is all sprung
And locked in the rust of inner change.
The therapist who plucks him like a harp
Is a cold torture: the animal bleats
And whimpers on its far seashore
As she leans to her find with a smooth hunger.

Somewhere in a storm my pity went down:
It was a wooden figurehead
With sea-hard breasts and polished mouth.
But women wash my friend with brine
From shallow inlets of their eyes,
And women rock my friend with waves
That pulsate from the female moon.
They gather at his very edge and haul
My driftwood friend toward their fires.

ISRAEL

When I think of the liberation of Palestine,
When my eye conceives the great black English line
Spanning the world news of two thousand years,
My heart leaps forward like a hungry dog,
My heart is thrown back on its tangled chain,
My soul is hangdog in a Western chair.

When I think of the battle for Zion I hear
The drop of chains, the starting forth of feet
And I remain chained in a Western chair.
My blood beats like a bird against a wall,
I feel the weight of prisons in my skull
Falling away; my forebears stare through stone.

When I see the name of Israel high in print
The fences crumble in my flesh; I sink
Deep in a Western chair and rest my soul.
I look the stranger clear to the blue depths
Of his unclouded eye. I say my name
Aloud for the first time unconsciously.

Speak of the tillage of a million heads
No more. Speak of the evil myth no more
Of one who harried Jesus on his way
Saying, *Go faster.* Speak no more
Of the yellow badge, *secta nefaria.*
Speak the name only of the living land.

THE LEG

Among the iodoform, in twilight-sleep,
What have I lost? he first inquires,
Peers in the middle distance where a pain,
Ghost of a nurse, hazily moves, and day,
Her blinding presence pressing in his eyes
And now his ears. They are handling him
With rubber hands. He wants to get up.

One day beside some flowers near his nose
He will be thinking, *When will I look at it?*
And pain, still in the middle distance, will reply,
At what? and he will know it's gone,
O where! and begin to tremble and cry.
He will begin to cry as a child cries
Whose puppy is mangled under a screaming wheel.

Later, as if deliberately, his fingers
Begin to explore the stump. He learns a shape
That is comfortable and tucked in like a sock.
This has a sense of humor, this can despise
The finest surgical limb, the dignity of limping,
The nonsense of wheel-chairs. Now he smiles to the wall:
The amputation becomes an acquisition.

For the leg is wondering where he is (all is not lost)
And surely he has a duty to the leg;
He is its injury, the leg is his orphan,
He must cultivate the mind of the leg,
Pray for the part that is missing, pray for peace
In the image of man, pray, pray for its safety,
And after a little it will die quietly.

The body, what is it, Father, but a sign
To love the force that grows us, to give back
What in Thy palm is senselessness and mud?
Knead, knead the substance of our understanding
Which must be beautiful in flesh to walk,
That if Thou take me angrily in hand
And hurl me to the shark, I shall not die!

May Swenson
(1913-   )

THE BLINDMAN

The blindman placed
a tulip on his tongue for purple's taste.
Cheek to grass, his green

was rough excitement's sheen
of little whips.
In water to his lips

he named the sea blue and white,
the basin of his tears and fallen beads of sight.
He said: This scarf is red;

I feel the vectors to its thread
that dance down from the sun. I know
the seven fragrances of the rainbow.

I have caressed
the orange hair of flames. Pressed
to my ear,

a pomegranate lets me hear
crimson's flute.
Trumpets tell me yellow. Only ebony is mute.

FABLE FOR WHEN THERE'S NO WAY OUT

Grown too big for his skin,
and it grown hard,

without a sea and atmosphere—
he's drunk it all up—

his strength's inside him now,
but there's no room to stretch.

He pecks at the top
but his beak's too soft;

though instinct and ambition shoves,
he can't get through.

Barely old enough to bleed
and already bruised!

In a case this tough
what's the use

if you break your head
instead of the lid?

Despair tempts him
to just go limp:

Maybe the cell's
already a tomb,

and beginning end
in this round room.

Still, stupidly he pecks
and pecks, as if from under

his own skull—
yet makes no crack . . .

No crack until
he finally cracks,

and kicks and stomps.
What a thrill

and shock to feel
his little gaff poke

through the floor!
A way he hadn't known or meant.

Rage works if reason won't.
When locked up, bear down.

FLYING HOME FROM UTAH

Forests are branches of a tree lying down,
its blurred trunk in the north.
Farms are fitted pieces of a floor,

tan and green tiles that get smoother,
smaller, the higher we fly.
Heel-shaped dents of water I know are deep

from here appear opaque, of bluish glass.
Curl after curl, rivers are coarse locks
unravelling southward over the land;

hills, rubbed felt, crumpled bumps
of antlers pricking from young bucks' heads.
Now towns are scratches here and there

on a wide, brown-bristled hide.
Long roads rayed out from the sores of cities
begin to fester and crawl with light—

above them the plane is a passing insect
that eyes down there remark, forget
in the moment it specks the overcast.

It climbs higher. Clouds become ground.
Pillows of snow meet, weld into ice.
Alone on a moonlit stainless rink

glides the ghost of a larva, the shadow
of our plane. Lights go on
in the worm-belly where we sit;

it becomes the world, and seems to cease
to travel—only vibrates, stretched out tense
in the tank of night.

The room of my mind replaces the long, lit room.
I dream I point my eye over a leaf
and fascinate my gaze upon its veins:

A sprawled leaf, many-fingered, its radial
ridges limber, green—but curled,
tattered, pocked, the brown palm

nibbled by insects, nestled in by worms:
One leaf of a tree that's one tree of a forest,
that's the branch of the vein of a leaf

of a tree. Perpetual worlds
within, upon, above the world, the world
a leaf within a wilderness of worlds.

William Stafford
(1914-   )

IN THE NIGHT DESERT

The Apache word for love stings
    then numbs the tongue:
Uttered once clear, said—
    never that word again.

"Cousin," you call, or "Sister" and one
    more word that spins
In the dust: a flake
    chipped like obsidian.

The girl who hears this flake and
    follows you into the dark
Turns at a touch: the night desert
    forever behind her back.

REPORT TO CRAZY HORSE

All the Sioux were defeated. Our clan
got poor, but a few got richer.
They fought two wars. I did not
take part. No one remembers your vision
or even your real name. Now
the children go to town and like
loud music. I married a Christian.

Crazy Horse, it is not fair
to hide a new vision from you.
In our schools we are learning
to take aim when we talk, and we have
found out our enemies. They shift when
words do; they even change and hide
in every person. A teacher here says
hurt or scorned people are places
where real enemies hide. He says
we should not hurt or scorn anyone,

but help them. And I will tell you
in a brave way, the way Crazy Horse
talked: that teacher is right.

I will tell you a strange thing:
at the rodeo, close to the grandstand,
I saw a farm lady scared by a blown
piece of paper; and at that place
horses and policemen were no longer
frightening, but suffering faces were,
and the hunched-over backs of the old.
Crazy Horse, tell me if I am right:
these are the things we thought we were
doing something about.

In your life you saw many strange things,
and I will tell you another: now I salute
the white man's flag. But when I salute
I hold my hand alertly on the heartbeat
and remember all of us and how we depend
on a steady pulse together. There are those
who salute because they fear other flags
or mean to use ours to chase them:
I must not allow my part of saluting
to mean this. All of our promises,
our generous sayings to each other, our
honorable intentions—these I affirm
when I salute. At these times it is like
shutting my eyes and joining a religious
colony at prayer in the gray dawn
in the deep aisles of a church.

Now I have told you about new times.
Yes, I know others will report
different things. They have been caught
by weak ways. I tell you straight
the way it is now, and it is our way,
the way we were trying to find.

The chokecherries along our valley
still bear a bright fruit. There is good
pottery clay north of here. I remember
our old places. When I pass the Musselshell
I run my hand along those old grooves in the rock.

IN THE OREGON COUNTRY

From old Fort Walla Walla and the Klickitats
to Umpqua near Port Orford, stinking fish tribes
massacred our founders, the thieving whites.

Chief Rotten Belly slew them at a feast;
Kamiakin riled the Snakes and Yakimas;
all spurted arrows through the Cascades west.

Those tribes became debris on their own lands:
Captain Jack's wide face above the rope,
his Modoc women dead with twitching hands.

The last and the most splendid, Nez Percé
Chief Joseph, fluttering eagles through Idaho,
dashed his pony-killing getaway.

They got him. Repeating rifles bored at his head,
and in one fell look Chief Joseph saw the game
out of that spiral mirror all explode.

Back of the Northwest map their country goes,
mountains yielding and hiding fold on fold,
gorged with yew trees that were good for bows.

Radcliffe Squires
(1917-   )

A DAY IN SALAMANCA

Across the square
The late sun angles down through arches
In golden cones against the violet
Shop windows. At a near table
A beautiful priest smiles at his expensive
Dessert; at another table, students, old-looking in
Their dark suits, talk erotically of revolution.
Then priest and students turn toward me with
The squint of conspirators.
While a boy, leaning into the slanted sunlight
As though it were wind, comes slowly
Across the immense square, tacking into the light,
Until he stands at my table.
His big wrists glow six inches
Beyond the scarecrow sleeves,
As he holds a sparrow toward me
And chants: "Which shall it be, freedom
Or blood-sacrifice?"
                    The bird peers
From the noose of thumb and forefinger,
Tightening to show the way of sacrifice.
I laugh. The boy scowls, his lips
Curl back from wet teeth. He pushes nearer,
A windowless smell of cooking oil comes
From his clothes, but beneath that, faintly,
The neutral perfume of all humanity, the smell
(I think) of wheat fields motionless in sunlight.
I lean back, shrug, and say he does not have
The courage to kill a bird. The insult brings
The moment we have all waited for. The priest
Titters, the students freeze. The boy's face,
Pressing nearer, blots out the square with
Its false sunset, whispering, *"Libertad o sacrificio?"*
And I drop the coin on the enameled table.

The bird spurts away like breath, but not far.
On a window ledge it waits, trying us
With one eye and then the other,
And when the boy whistles it comes to his hand.
From under his jacket he takes the small
Cage filigreed from pale clean wood,
A Moorish bower where the bird enters
Like a spoiled princess.

The priest and the students, bored now, turn away,
But the boy and I smile at each other,
Not decently nor gratefully, but with a certain love.
Each day now for a week I have bought
This same bird's life from this same boy
At this same table.
                    Why not?
The century being the century it is,
The role is a role worth perfecting.

STORM IN THE DESERT

No one has ever said he goes "out" into the city.
We always say we go out into the desert.
It is out; out of self, out of presences.
Absence is what we have here.
In deserts we stand under something
That is not there, a sea, a mountain.
And we feel it, but, whether it is prophecy
Or memory, we cannot say. We only know
The absence is waiting for something stranger
Than the future, more familiar than the past.

Look, the storm rises as a lavender
Light around these stopes whose grief
For something that is not there
Is the more bitter for the pale ungrieving
Springtime of their color. They are
Earth's ancient children, and though
They stand in the colors of leaf buds
They have longed for centuries to break.

As we enter the pass beyond them they still stand
In the old positions of their children's game.
A weary copper gleam of lightning
Flexes—the breaking of a guitar string—
And the storm comes over us. It is all the light
Of beginning one moment, then the black
Clot of time crushed, light shuddering
Again into dark again.
And if we look hard at the rain it is standing
Still, and the cliffs are rising through it.
The sea is here again; mountains are rising above us.

But they rise into a sky breaking into
Ordinary blue with a little hot jewel of sun.
The water runs away in the orderly whorls
Of stone-fingerprints, and small brown birds,
Jerking in the gravel, emit thin songs. Below us
In the valley those pale tall stopes
Stretch vernal-green, vernal-rose all the way
To the horizon. They are quite unchanged.
The storm's rhetoric, the civil grammar of the birds
Were only interruptions in their love of a vast absence.

VERMILION CLIFFS

The sun, they say, is dying. True, the pulse
Of that life so pure that it kills
Has grown debonair. But the sun's beginning
Was only a beginning and its ending
Will be only an end. That is the way
Of suns—and ourselves. There is also a state
That is neither beginning nor end, and it
Is greater than we and greater than suns. Ponder
These red cliffs that hang, mile after mile in Arizona—
I was going to say "that hang like a wave of blood

Frozen as a warning over the mammals' world." But that's
Not it. The cliffs are not blood. They are the harder stone,
The harder red, that stands when the soft is gone
Down trivial veins with the rain. Toward them,
Rather than the sun, it seems each cactus turns,
Discrete in its sleeve of light. And if we knew how stones
Turn, we should see that they, too, train
Themselves toward the cliffs. Shall we also turn
With them to find what is there whether sun shines
Or darkness shines, and with stones slowly feel
Ourselves become a body inhabiting a soul?

Clinton F. Larson
(1919-   )

HOMESTEAD IN IDAHO

I

"Solomon? Since I talked with him I've thought
Again about trying to make a go of it
In Idaho. As I say, this rainy weather
In Oregon is looking better and better to me.
The first time I met him, it was in Al's Bar,
Down the street. Five years ago, I think.
Well, you know, Al keeps a friendly place,
One where you don't mind stepping in
And acting neighborly. Well, there he was,
Down at the end of the bar. I noticed him
Because he was shaking, folding and unfolding a clipping.
'You from these parts?' I said. With all this space
In the West, it doesn't hurt to close it up
Whenever you can. He said, 'Well, no, not really,'
And kept folding and unfolding the clipping and looking
Down at his hands. When he stopped, I could hardly
See it, his hands were so square and big,
Like the farm work of his time. Besides, he took
His hat off, and you could see the white skin
Of his head, particularly near the part,
Where his hat took a settled, permanent place.
But his face had lightened to a buckskin color.
He had the look of a farmer who had seen a lot
Of land that needed working. Then it rose
From him. 'I suppose you would say from Idaho.
I wanted to homestead there,' he said. 'I tried it
Last year, or was it then? Not much money
To start with, but my wife Geneva and I and our children
Found a place. But it seemed a thousand miles
From nowhere, at least two weeks east from here.
I built a cabin from the boards I had brought
Along. Geneva said, 'Solomon, we can make it,
But we need money for spring. Go back to Tamarack
And leave us here.' Then I told her how I felt.

But she said, 'We can make it with the provisions we brought.
Go back, Solomon. By spring, we'll have a start,
Then a barn by those trees, cows grazing there,
And a house like we've wanted, beside a stream.'
Well, the way she looked, her eyes imploring,
And her soft brown hair, and her hope, how could I
Say no? So off I went, Geneva waving to me
Until I was out of sight. It was the hardest thing
I have ever done to look around and see
Where I was going. I worked at Tamarack
Autumn and winter, numb from wondering
How they were, all alone out there, and wanting
To get back to them. April finally came,
And I loaded the wagon with everything we needed,
Dresses and dry goods, shoes and ribbons besides.
I travelled as hard as I could, considering the horses,
And kept looking and looking for the smoke far off
In front of me, coming from the chimney,
To tell me I was near. But I never saw it.'
He looked again at the clipping in his hands,
Smudged and yellow, and said, 'When I got there,
It looked like autumn and winter had never left,
The snow still hanging on the roof, the door
Open, nothing planted, nothing done,
And then I went inside, to see the dusty cribs
And Geneva, still against them . . . and the floor
Red and dusted with shadows. And I was here,
Trying for money so we could get started. . . .
I couldn't stay out there.' And he looked at me
As if pleading for help, then down into his hands,
Unfolding and folding the clipping as if by doing it
He could wear out his sorrow."

II
The colors of the sun against the hills
In the evensong of life, and yet another
Year had gone. The colors crept down
Like frost and the glory of God, intermingling
In them night and day. All was over
When the family saw them, over like the evening
Wind. In the meadows and clusters of pines

It whispered to the edge of the sullen earth,
In the seethe of knowing, under the shaken plume
Of knowledge. Solomon and Geneva saw
The land cut, as it were, for them, a place
For them between the great divide and the sea.
There, he said in the voice of conscience, there
Is our home, or the hope of it. Geneva,
Can it be that home if we settle here?
A half of a year will make it ours if we stay,
She replied in the moment of seeing him
As she wished him to be. And then in resolve,
Let me stay the winter with the children
While you work in Tamarack, and so
It was out, the only way of keeping
The land. Where in the flicker of grey is death,
The wandering light, release? I want this home,
She said, in the tolerance of a breath, and I
Shall stay. Where is the imperious will but fast
Against the land that holds them? To Tamarack,
He said, bright as possession, like the coin of having
Mastery. There is my knoll where home
Shall be, not this cabin of our duration
As we should not be, itinerants in hope of more.
A winter more, she said, and it is ours,
The gaze of meadows, the water and soil
Urgent for grain, the quiet sky, and the light
Lazy as spring. Our home! And I shall keep it,
Winter through, she said, as if it were no winter,
But a day of rest. And then beside him, their children,
Or in his arms, awake to happiness. The future
Declined from that day and would not rest,
But as a bole of pain grew into that tower
Of resolve and broke it easily, sacred
As a sacrifice. He said, then think of me
In Tamarack, and turned to what he needed
Away from home. Geneva? The subtle portrait
On a stand beside a bed. The wisps
Of hair she flicked to clear her face, brown
As the veil of earth, eyes quizzical as worry,
But light as a soft morning, her body lithe
And restless, supple to the rule of God.

And Solomon? A name like a fetish he tried
To honor, but not as a patriarch, more
Like a seer: angular as a fence or cross,
Bending as he seemed to fit, concern
Like an agony to please, a burden
To his clothes that could not shape themselves,
And altogether like the square largeness
Of his hands. Together, they kept the cabin
Like a tidy loom where they would weave
The colors through their bright fidelity.
Their children? Hard to presuppose or know,
But theirs. Such small alliances, wont
To shimmer with translucent light, a guess
Of women that might have been, of course like her,
Or him, as others might suppose, not they.
She whispered what he might take, advice
Hanging from her words like surety.
And he, the slight concerns of food and health
Like the hundreds of miles that would intervene,
And for safety the gun and knife in a drawer,
Nearby. Then the wood for winter near the door,
Neatly stacked, and provisions in the loft
And ready. What else? What else but land
Beyond their vision, the canyons, and peaks like clouds
In the thin blue haze, and time. He turned, ready,
Holding her with one arm, as he pulled
His horse from grazing to the suggestion of the miles
Ahead, and leaned to kiss his children, and then
Away, easily in the saddle, gazing back at her,
The children, cabin, everything diminishing
As he moved, and he waved, and they, in the slow
Desperation of goodbye. He could not turn forward
For seeing them there, until they were taken from view
By a vale beyond their meadow sinking into darkness,
And they were gone. From that time on he pieced
The events of time together like fragments he could not
Understand, though the evidence impaled the past
Like needles dropping suddenly through his inquiry.
There must have been a disturbance beyond the door,
And she left the cabin with the gun on her arm,
The sharp wind of October against her frailty

Where she shivered in the grey dusk. The rising
Wind, then the thunder over the plain that shook her.
She went into the darkness of a shed, wildly
Gazing. Then the severe and immediate rattle
Behind her, and the strike behind her knee, the prongs
Of venom there that made her scream. Now
The whirling thoughts for Solomon or help
From anywhere. Bleed the poison out.
Go slowly, she told herself, and bleed the poison
Out. Stumbling to the cabin, she opened the door
In the glaze of fright and found the drawer that held
The knife. She sat, livid against the lightning,
To find the place to cut. Nowhere to see,
Behind and under, but she felt the red periods there.
A piece of kindling for a brace, a cloth
For tourniquet. She took the knife and swept it
With her hand. But the chickens in the shed.
They must not starve. A few steps back
To the shed, and she emptied a pail of grain
And opened the door. As she moved, she held
The stick of the tourniquet numbly against her leg.
Slowly, slowly to the cabin, then wildly in
To seize the knife. She held it against her leg
And with a gasp twisted it in. But too deep!
The blood pulsed against her hand, again,
Again, no matter how tightly she twisted the stick
To keep it in. It spread on the rough floor
As she felt herself weaken, the waves of blackness
Before her eyes. The children! What will happen
To them? she cried to herself. The lamp flickered
At the sill. What good is the need and planning now?
Tears for dust. The girls will starve to death
In the clatter of the wind, and the light of afternoon
Will carve through their sallow loneliness.
They will lie here and cry for food, and no one will hear.
The waning fire, the gusts at the filming window.
Solomon! Forgive me! What can I do?
What else can I do? She took the gun again
And turned it to the crib, propping its weight.
She looked at them as they slept, arms lightly
Across each other. You will be with me

She whispered to them. The trigger once, then again,
The flat sounds walling her against the error
That they would live beyond her careful dying.
The gun fell from her. She crawled to the bed
In the corner and, taking her finger, traced
In blood on the white sheet, "Rattlesnake bit,
Babies would starv—" and the land fell away
Beyond her sight, and all that she was collapsed
In an artifice of death that he afterwards saw.
Solomon!

TO A DYING GIRL

How quickly must she go?
She calls dark swans from mirrors everywhere:
From halls and porticos, from pools of air.
How quickly must she know?
They wander through the fathoms of her eye,
Waning southerly until their cry
Is gone where she must go.
How quickly does the cloudfire streak the sky,
Tremble on the peaks, then cool and die?
She moves like evening into night,
Forgetful as the swans forget their flight
Or spring the fragile snow,
So quickly she must go.

ADVENT

The gentle God is our guest:
His staff will prompt us to the door.

The table is set in the oak-paneled room:
Goblets are rinsed and set out,
The warm vapor vanishing around them:
The silver, withdrawn from felt-lined red mahogany,
Is counted and burnished to mercurial white
And set on immaculate linen,
Sleek with crystal and rococo ware.

The table is set for the Guest
Near the imminent door.
The servants stalk
Each gray indiscretion to be rent
On the merciless rack of their decor.

The table is set for the gentle God:
The roasted fowl entice the savoring tongue:
The marmalade and sweetmeats brim
The centerpiece, a horn:
The fruit is full, plucked in prime,
Oranges, apples, pears
Like noon-shade autumn leaves.
The supper will please the gentle God
Who surely comes,
Who comes like the breath on a veil.

But out of the East the breath is fire!
Who comes with temblor, sound of hurricane?
Who rages on the portico?
Who claps his vengeful steel on stone?
Who comes to dine?

The servants cower like quail in the anterooms.
Who blasphemes in the shuddering halls?
Who rends the imminent door?
Our guest is a gentle God, a Lamb.

CACTUS STEM

Once white with bells, and blithe, but now a mast
Tan with spars above the tiny tassels of blades,
The tall stem of cactus barely tips, fast
In the moraine, erect. The wind vanes and fades,
An aria over shadows of clouds, and then
From a nook of history, a sheet of newsprint
Flies against it and stays, as if from a fen
Of being, caught and balanced by the dint
Of chance. But now the stalk is tipsy spastic,
As if death were near, tremulo and cadenza
Brightening with fury, uncontrollable and elastic,
Shuddering against the high wind's bonanza
Of gilding air, the sailing spectre of madness
There and there, shaken and lithe in its sadness.

SEVEN-TENTHS OF A SECOND

There's the tree, shaded and stolid as death,
And you, in the impress of speed, a mile a minute
On a register, weigh forward with your last breath
To note in a curious gravity the casual limit

Of an illusion pressing you to settle still
Foward at three thousand, two hundred pounds.
In the compression the bumper flows into the grill,
And its bits of steel slip into the tree with sounds

Of puncturing; the hood rises and waves into the shield
In front of you as the drive of wheels lifts and hovers,
Twisting openly; the grill spills its flakes, annealed
Into colors of light; the body steel covers

The trunk as if a casual mantle sloping in
And corresponding; and the rear enfolds and splays
The doors that move like tongues floating in
A discourse of the day. Your body plays

Against its speed as the structures near you
Brake you easily: your legs reach straight,
Snap at the knees, leaping short, and shear you
At the groin; off the seat, your torso like a crate

Settles into the dashboard as your chest and arm
Curve the steering wheel; you crest into the visor,
Though you cannot see the pitching motor block harm
The chipping trunk, for you keep speed, wiser

Than before without knowing; the steering column
Bends vertical, and you, driven and impaled,
Fail inwardly, pulsing blood into your solemn
Lungs. Your head is mantled and assailed

With glass. The car reclines into the ground,
Conforming noisily as hinges rip, doors pry
And rail the air, and seats rise, puff, and bound
Forward to press and pin you where you die.

Madeline DeFrees
(1919-   )

IN THE SCALES: I
from "A Catch of Summer"

July dust covers the ever-
greens where I lie, heavy
with summer, lost in the opaque cry
of the owl drowned in day. Or wake
to the nightly blare of the great
horned moon and the grave sinking
of stars. There in the full hour
I go to meet my time and gauge
the drop from a ledge of light into
sleep. The hand rounds on my shoulder,
ticks in my finger ends, follows
the slow blood to the crack in the wall
till I knock on the dull disposition
of bodies, casting the weather
of all that weight and, deliberate,
turn my face to the fall.

IN THE SCALES: II

from "A Catch of Summer"

At halfpast summer when the creek
bed runs dry downhill and the
rolling stone outwits the law
to shed its gravity every
thing turns to straw:

foxtail grass that took the sun in
chase, green in the turning light or
red, disheveled and whiskery now;
toadflax sprawling and spurred
to the finish; tumbleweed

skirt over head, blowzy and blown;
the best gone to seed, pressed in a pod;
on hollow stalks dead or in husks
mocked up, their powdery charms sifted
like butterflies racked.

And bachelor buttons stuck
with their sense of form
through a colorless time.

HOPE DIAMONDS

One hundred fifty miles down, these uncut
faces of stone drill towards light.
The odds in gravel and sand, one hundred million
to one. In Kimberley's basic rock, fourteen
million. Miners down on their luck call this
blue ground. Know the curse that follows thieves
and rich owners all the way back to the stolen eye
of an idol. Still they will work sixteen years
for a flash of that blue fire to polarize light,
believing the lode more than hard weight,
steel-blue in a self-inflicted wound. Or the captain's
greed that lowered a slave's dead body like a drowned
cat. They count on crystals fat as a fist
dug out with a penknife more than on carbon they burn
as they tunnel towards black lung.
                         I suppose I could
learn to play oyster, coat minor irritations
with cultured pearls. Forget unbelievable pressures—
a million pounds to the square inch—and heat
too intense to imagine. Except for the unlucky shah
who died under torture refusing to give up the stone
of his father. The Brahman priest in exile. Or the star
of the Folies Bergère done in by a jealous lover.
The diamond brought from Lahore to Queen Victoria.
That Greek broker driven off a windy cliff with his wife
and sons. The mines near Pretoria. Consider Marie
Antoinette moving her jewels aside for the blade
and the gaudy American millionairess smuggled into
the harem to look, who paid by installment—first
money, then a husband gone mad and two children.

Recovery is rare at these levels, the shape of twin
pyramids touching bases more real than a wake.
The lure, the lore of the hidden. Every side
of refractory matter splitting light. Excited
atoms cooled to latticed arrangement. A deep
blaze waiting to surface. Bribe, ransom, dowry,
wage. The burning faces near as the constant desert.

"MY DREAM OF PURE INVENTION"

Nothing comes to a halt sleeping off
the highway. There is snow
on the ground in Harrisburg. Icicles hang
from eaves
the tired scenes unreel. Night comes
into its own
sidewalk cafes. The white safaris
open wings
in the Oriental Pyrenees. We seed the clouds
waiting for our lives
to fall on us. The marriage in Mexico a rumor
all that summer.

Around a potbellied stove
our hands warm
we check the positions of stars
pinned against the storm windows,
double back
towards Plum Creek where cattle drowse
in their snowy stalls.
All roads closed.

Remember winter in Berlin, the places we have been
together.
The bamboo forest
darkness whistles through,
travel folder lies
opened like accordions. The moon, too,
that first disturber of sleep.
This broken day an early sun recalls
the hands, everything cheap when we pretend
pulling away from the body.

WATCH FOR FALLEN ROCK

Seeing the coyote flash across the road,
outcrop of stone, the fawn shy among
reluctant green, I can entertain the Amazon
virgin on the ship's prow bearing down.
Remember how, wave after wave, the overwhelming
line from hip to ankle determined that
foreshortened figure. Unlike the bronze pope
destroyed, she never stayed where air was too thin
for the sea's germane reflections. Her wooden image
sent me back to gather rock roses in the canyon.
Porcelain petals flared like bones. A herd
of grasses rippled over the cliff. Where winter
had opposed black ice in all the passes, it was
as if those toppled urns outside our coastal
window let the sea disguise what sun could not
set fire to. In surprising turns the road signs missed,
ghosts of antelope and elk might glow
an instant in our headlights and go under
while at home we watched the deer and frost
move in to claim our bronze chrysanthemums.

WITH A BOTTLE OF BLUE NUN TO ALL MY FRIENDS

I

Sisters,
The Blue Nun has eloped with one
of the Christian Brothers. They are living
in a B&B Motel just out of
Sacramento.

II
The Blue Nun works the late shift
in Denver. Her pierced ears
drip rubies
like the Sixth Wound.

III
This is to inform you
that the Blue Nun
will become Mayor of Missoula
in the new dispensation.
At fifty-eight she threw her starched coif
into the ring and was off to a late win
over Stetson and deerstalker,
Homburg and humbug,
Church and State.

IV
When you receive this you will know
that the Blue Nun
has blacked out
in a sleazy dive
outside San Francisco.
They remember her in Harlem.
She still carried her needle case
according to the ancient custom.

V
You may have noticed
how the walls lean towards the river
where a veil of fog hides a sky diver's
pale descent. The parachute
surrounds her like a wimple.
That's what happens when Blue Nuns
bail out.
It's that simple.

THE FAMILY GROUP

from "Figures for a Carrousel"

That Sunday at the zoo I understood the child
I never had would look like this: stiff-fingered
spastic hands, a steady drool and eyes in cages
with a danger sign. I felt like stone myself,
the ancient line curved inward in a sunblind
stare. My eyes were flat. Flat eyes for tanned
young couples with their picture-story kids.

Heads turned our way but you'd learned not to care.
You stood tall as Greek columns, weather-streaked
face bent toward the boy. I wanted to take his hand,
hallucinate a husband. He whimpered at my touch.
You watched me move away and grabbed my other
hand as much in love as pity for our land-
locked town. I heard the visionary rumor of the sea.

What holds the three of us together in my mind
is something no one planned. The chiseled look of mutes.
A window shut to keep out pain. Wooden blank
of doors. That stance the mallet might surprise if it
could strike the words we hoard for fears galloping
at night over moors through convoluted bone.
The strange uncertain rumor of the sea.

DRIVING HOME

The wheels keep pulling
towards that sunny sideroad.
I pull them back, headed for Blue Creek.
Grasses getting thin, the rushes lean. Nothing here
the wind can use against me.

In the long stretch
after Cataldo takes the hill, I think about
Clarence Worth Love's annulment
till a nerve gives way.
The gradual curve unwinds
the river again. Now it is green in the placid
crook of my arm
as the paired hands of those days
I wanted to die.

By the Superior exit
the highway crew leaves markers
I do not trust. The diamond
watch for crossing game, for ice and rocks,
hangs a legend on my lights.
I do the same. One star is out to get me.

A level sound. Pastures graze the trees
around the shoulder.
On a high beam, the mare swings
her dark side to the moon.
Something turns over in the trunk.
I think
one more time
of your black luggage
on the bed. I know
it may not carry me much longer.

Ann Stanford
(1921-   )

THE BLACKBERRY THICKET

I stand here in the ditch, my feet on a rock in the water,
Head-deep in a coppice of thorns,
Picking wild blackberries,
Watching the juice-dark rivulet run
Over my fingers, marking the lines and the whorls,
Remembering stains—
The blue of mulberry on the tongue
Brown fingers after walnut husking,
And the green smudge of grass—
The earnest part
Of heat and orchards and sweet springing places.
Here I am printed with the earth
Always and always the earth ground into the fingers,
And the arm scratched in thickets of spiders.
Over the marshy water the cicada rustles,
A runner snaps sharp into place.
The dry leaves are a presence,
A companion that follows up under the trees of the orchard
Repeating my footsteps. I stop to listen.
Surely not alone
I stand in this quiet in the shadow
Under a roof of bees.

THE WHITE HORSE

Where is the white horse?
I asked the toyon and the walnuts.
The toyon was flowering,
The walnuts lifted their leaves lightly like feathers.
They were tossing and flowering and the wind rustled a little.
It was dark there under the trees.

I tried the meadow.
Where is the white horse
I asked the mustard and rye grass,
Have you seen her?
The mustard was yellow and the rye going to seed.
I could tell the old horse had been there.
She had left her mementos.

Where is the white horse?
I asked the towhees down by the corral.
They looked at me sideways.
One had already drowned in the water trough.
The birds had little to say. The corral was deserted.

I walked past the toyon and walnuts
And over the meadow and up the hill.
I knew the white horse had been there.
She's lame, I said. *she can't go far.*
And I went up the road to the next stable.
There was only a black horse and a brown one.
They tossed their manes on the wind and kicked their heels a little.

Where is the white horse, I said.
She was here yesterday.

HIDDEN THINGS

1

Upon the wall, drawn by a child's hand,
The horses twitch their tails or clash their hooves
In formal duel in an unreal land.
And they are sealed in stillness, though all moves

About them. No one sees them paw the air
For they are painted over, and no stain
Shows where they fly. Yet certainly they are there.
They are secret as the packet sealed with chain

To the courier's wrist, and even more, for none
Shall read what codes this flying herd might bring.
And so they stretch in their impenetrable zone.

2

Beneath engulfments of ocean, ground, and green

Between the lid of the box and the enclosed
Or the layers of paint or leaf, under sheared surfaces,
The hidden things broaden and are disposed
As rounded bodies in immeasurable space.

As gold beaten to foil may yet endure
Another stroke, and thin and thin again
So does each changing layer yield but more
The wheels and chambers of the finest plane.

No violence attains these inward stores.
Nor the slow fall of stealth, or shifts of day
Complete their rendezvous, although we shower
Echo with roar and labor. Suddenly

We are within the sound that we have made,
Within the box, and mystery surrounds
With vacancies of sun, enclosing shade
Of articulate blue. It is no simple ground

On which we walk, but treasuries of roots
And stones and hollow chambers, and the slow
Descent of parting things.   How lonely broods
The orchard, raising the green whispering show

Of summer through the roofs of cottages,
Through lawns and asphalt, in incorrigible tiers,
Remembered seasons, and beyond, in that place,
The waving grass of time's old furniture.

3

What lies beneath the terrace of flesh, the pale
Secluding forehead, in that weir of past
Illusions or hoped events? I cannot tell:
As one walks in darkness past a house

Suffused with radiance, and the curtains pulled
And curious, waits, discovers there a sum
Of uncovered light and finds within revealed
A shadow passing from the empty room.

But could I go within where dark and gold
Lean close together, hear the voices' tremor,
Still I would be outside each separate world
Illumined by its own conservator.

Alas, poor Psyche, did you think the fire,
The quick uncovering of the lamp would prove
By adding sight, the death of your desire?
You only changed unknown, for loss of, love.

4

Last night, happy and clear, I saw the dead.
We walked together over a wide lawn,
The living not more real than those dear shades,
And leaving to wake, I said farewell again.

Day world of birdsong, when I woke in light
And resonant morning, could any thought distress
This clear existence, paced by breath and bright
Air in which I move. For surfaces

Are hard, and depth the clean repeating of
The seen. The scene cut through and every leaf the same,
A chord of agate, into which we move.
The immortal hardening of a mortal plane.

Yet in this plain, by every light we sense
We lose as much, slipped back into that bend
Of suffering's waste, unrecollected suns—
Lose, and behold only the figured mind,

The dreamed, annihilable soul, psyche
Beyond the surface of the face, and there
Secretly rest. Where absolute abides
Abide all secret things, in an unbroken care.

DOUBLE MIRROR

As this child rests upon my arm
So you encircled me from harm,
And you in turn were held by her
And she by her own comforter.

Enclosed, the double mirror runs
Backward and forward, fire to sun.
And as I watch you die, I hear
A child's farewell in my last ear.

THE BEATING

The first blow caught me sideways, my jaw
Shifted. The second beat my skull against my
Brain. I raised my arm against the third.
Downward my wrist fell crooked. But the sliding

Flood of sense across the ribs caught in
My lungs. I fell for a long time,
One knee bending. The fourth blow balanced me.
I doubled at the kick against my belly.

The fifth was light. I hardly felt the
Sting. And down, breaking against my side, my
Thighs, my head. My eyes burst closed, my
Mouth the thick blood curds moved through. There

Were no more lights. I was flying. The
Wind, the place I lay, the silence.
My call came to a groan. Hands touched
My wrist. Disappeared. Something fell over me.

Now this white room tortures my eye.
The bed too soft to hold my breath,
Slung in plaster, caged in wood.
Shapes surround me.

No blow! No blow!
They only ask the thing I turn
Inside the black ball of my mind,
The one white thought.

THE LATE VISITOR

Listen, let me explain, it was not the fire
That burned in the hearth and kept me there.
It was no real fire, though I swear it did seem so
And to go out was to step into blackest snow,
And to stay was to lose, not find. Words only say
What is gone. Or are motions like flame and snow,
Slow circlings of something about to occur,
The birth of a salamander in the fire.

I am caught between never and now. You must tell me to go.

WEEDS

Nothing so startles us as tumbleweeds in December
Rising like ghosts before us in the headlamps
The big round weeds blowing into fences
Into guard rails and wheels, wedged into corners
Drifting in ranks over roads in a gusty order
Round in the orbits of winter, dropping the invisible seed,
Blown green and purple-leaved into springtime, soft with water,
Filled to harsh circles in the thirsty summer
Dried brown and jagged, ready for December
When the silver globes, magnificent in procession
Slow and solemn-paced in the ritual of ending
Dry, dead, in the dim-most part of the year
Spread the great round promises of green morning.

THE ARTIST UNDERGROUND

I had that one great longing to behold the sphere of the sun.
—Benvenuto Cellini

They shoved me into the hole. Under
My feet the rustling away of small creatures.
I tried to see. I thought the sound
Was the stepping of rats. No light
Except an hour or two at midday, when the sun
Lit on a grey wall somewhere above.

Water, a stink of it, seeped from above,
Not much, but it wet the dirt under
My mattress of straw. It molded. The passing sun
Showed me the iron door that kept me, the creatures
That shared my cell. Centipedes. Spiders that hid from the
                                        light
In corners. I heard them walk; there was no other sound.

I learned how a world without sound
Lay under the stone of the courtyard above
Lay like the dark under the light
Sides of the leaves. And in this under-
World was a myriad of dark-haunting creatures
Cringing away from even that weak hour of sun.

I thought of the waste of all that sun
Lying everywhere. And the exuberance of sound—
Wheels turning. Metal clanging. The rooster waking
                              all creatures.
Laughter. Dogs. The street, alive. Above,
Me, next to the garden, horses, harness creaking. Here, under,
I grew used to the silence, the pale passing of light.

My eyes grew wide. Like a mole out of light
I could see the damp wall of my cage. The sun
Was my desire. But I rejoiced that under
The earth in this bare place, the sound
Of my prayers echoed. They spring straight above.
I thanked God for the life of his creatures.

And in that dark I was in the company of creatures
Greater than man. One led me to the light.
I had longed to see it in the world above
To look once again on the whole sun
A blaze so enormous it came as a sound
Nearly unbearable breaking into my dungeon there under.

And with the creatures of day I entered the sun
Whose light shines out through all things of the upper world.
                              Its sound
The canticles of all above rooted in that praise deep under.

A. Wilber Stevens
(1921-   )

IF YOU SHOULD DIE

If you should die in my house
I will be afraid of the wind which brought you
When they take you down the stairs evenly
And deposit you like cotton in the car
And then take you down again to take your blood
I will know my house is not right for me.

I cannot bring you back again
And if this banal truth is true you should not die
You should not die at least in my house
Where there is a speaking tube and an old piano
And where people once sang at evenings
And where my father lay dead to receive my child kiss.

If you should die in my house
And if there were an ocean near my window lights
I would crawl on my roof and fly over the strapped thing
They use to take people like you to lower rooms
Those tax free rooms full of silence and sirens and coffee
Where already I lie dead with you cold and stone and true.

AND ONE OTHER THING

I should have died a Trojan or a Spartan
Or someone mechanical or full of deadly machines
I keep seeing the more morbid side of things
When you get right down to it really
I should have been a headwaiter or a good lover
Or a Chairman preferably of someone else's Board
I keep wondering—perhaps a quiet doctor
Charging a lot and never saying much.

I should have died Established or at least Taboo
Instead I leave my card and shun the Out-Of-Doors
And wonder why I should have died not being
That very Thing I should have been whether
Secluded in some New Hampshire village waging
Wisdom or perhaps wondering bitter things
Oh so sullen Things in a desert someplace where
I could have died complete and whole and all alone.

ANOTHER POEM ON THE TEARING DOWN OF
THE METROPOLITAN OPERA HOUSE

Who has seen the old baritone of my childhood?
The one on Stage Left who was fat and alone
And sang Verdi as if he owned him and as if
Nobody nobody at all was around to tell him
That he was in the chorus of a tired opera
And that he was neither Milton Cross nor a lesser saint.

Where is the baritone of my childhood, the
Old Baritone I used to see (I think) leaving onto
The avenue then down to the subway with a copy of the
News tucked away in an abused coat on a bitter night?
Once in *Aida* he shook his fist at the audience
During an otherwise bland matinee oh fine oh fine.

WOOD WALK

To gather the wood with a hard eye
The visual thing in the sun
This is making the major remark
Pulling gently from the earth
Fitting idea into the hand
Listening for what is seen
This is to gather the real ruins
The remnants of all tugs-of-war
Walk around the tutelary mountain
Really touch then carry
Really touch wood have a land
Talk alone see the lovely cold air.

TRENDS AND CONDITIONS: MISCELLANEOUS FILE

So fell behind his day
He was good often for morning things
He penned his game and talked
He never left dust on his table.

His heart held fairly well
He was loved by a few quiet people
He ate alone in the middle evening,
He was attuned to the terror of friends.

If he had known his madness
He would have told no one
For he liked to feel in a diffident way
That only God sensed the death of his dream.

Now that the digging is done
And we have mounted his tears on our slides
We can return to matters of the unborn
And the careful killing of new wonders.

CRITIC UNDEFILED

This random blood affronts my pensive day
The unfilled gourd of hope assails my knees
I walk stone cold on streets of proper trees
I hear all children quarrel in the clay.

I hold my neutered books against the air
The treasuries of rupture shade my sun
The bells of tired insight bagged and hung
Decoy my fear and cauterize my prayer.

A saint can build a box-kite with his sins
And hold his shriven pity by a string
But grounded and appeased I sorely bring
My dear dead wit to school and paint with pins.

John Williams
(1922-   )

ACCESSIONS TO AUTUMN

I

Another summer is gone; sumac
reddens, pods stiffen on stalks, berries
glisten on bare bushes, and the air
has burnished its meanest possession
to something like a newness. Autumn
is rhetoric, a cold far wind that
blows the riot of decay upon
an earth that is loose, open beyond
all passion, and will take whatever
enters down to its roots. I will not
say that this is false. But look! there is
wonder here beyond analogy
and beyond all save the dim language
that struggles upward out of the poem.

II

It is no journey; age goes
through one until one is tired,
and it ceases. Thus, in my
garden in a cold autumn
I am moved by a going
that holds apart two crises,
and I have no concern for
the old distractions, the far
irrelevancies that fix
before and after. Here, late
peonies burst like moons in
the shadows; the leaves are plump
in a last ripeness; there is
nothing here that will endure
the crisis of another

season—except memory,
that fixes in its abstract
light parodies of what has
been, and waits in a solemn
innocence to be fulfilled.

III
In the bare autumn,
under a soft sky,
leaves fall; and this leaf
in the hand quickens
what has been, what is,
and what is to come.
Now memory is
irrevocable
and briefly unstill,
and the past merely
what it might have been,
the aggregate of
disembodied wants,
the dim prophecy
of now, the portent
of what is to be.
And the withered leaf
crumbles from the hand
and falls unmeaning
to the simple earth,
its dark accession.

IV
Potentiality, a lean ghost,
follows me like a shadow, darkening
what is. Who would know the promise it
devises? the flesh it would fulfill?
In the bright casuistry of a late
October sun, I look at the shape
of an identity that moves as
I move on the ground and mocks my flesh
with an unsubstantial perfection—
until the light fails, and distinctions
go down into the dark, and I sit

alone in the quick solidity
of my self, looking at a blankness
as if I were no longer haunted.

V

Who shall be judge of the brief
discourse that is myself? Not
the disembodiment of
my childhood whose far cold voice
measured my dreaming; and not
the faceless abstraction of
my fellows, now and to come,
who celebrate endlessly
rituals of illusion,
conceiving themselves; no, nor
my own self, that parody
of all the otherness it
can imagine: not these, but
you, the lone reader, whom I
shall never see, you who sit
in a pause of distraction,
alone in a familiar
room, drinking cold coffee,
who move upon these dry words
from your own odd angle, caught
by a passion that has come
between us for a moment.

PASSAGE

Below the terrace where he sits
A cloudless blue spills out the sea
And flings it hissing on the shore;
Flings it, recedes, and flings again
White foam on foam till foam is thrust
By its own weight into the sand.
A dark gull claws the summer air,
Whose brightness tips one wheeling wing.

An old man nods in the summer sun
And dreams that in such radiance is
His past. Forest, mountain, plain;
Volcanic rock of liquid ash;
The trackless paths that led him here—
What are they now? It seems that they
Are nothing. The slow years wash
And sink like foam in the mirage
That is the journey of his youth.

He thinks: Are there no mountains of
The human mind, where aspens stir
In casual winds, streams wear on rocks
And pulse with hungry fish, where drought
Is coldly abrupt at timberline?
And he remembers: Once aspen paled
To gold where mountains darkened, trout
Flicked silver in the frothing streams,
And limber pine whispered in hard
Cold passion to the winter sun.
And dreams it was his restless eye
Roved in such passion over stream
And tree and over those white peaks
That rimmed to blue, and hollowed in
Hot sand valleys fertile and rife
With damping springs. Roved, and returned
To where he stood. His naked boot,
Sullen to rock, impervious
And numb, gouged in the solid earth.
He stayed to see no season turn,
Nor clod break in the driving rain,
Nor mountain torn to rivulet,
To stream, at last to tumbling gorge.

Something beyond that wilderness
Has brought him here, at last, upon
This combed-out, soft Pacific sand—
Some urging of the blood that seeks
Its primal urge, the blind salt pounding
Ceaselessly upon the shore,
Out of the dark and landless deep.

An old man sits in the summer sun,
And in its glow his shadow lengthens
Where he cannot see. It creeps
Beyond the sand, it gathers rock
And eucalyptus tree, it drifts
Through labyrinths of brick and steel
In glutted cities, and beyond.
He waits in time. In the thickening west
The level sea flares to the sun
Before his shadow and the shade are one.

Kenneth O. Hanson
(1922-   )

SNOW

after Lin Ho-ching

Eight
a.m. with the doors
and windows drifted shut—
how could there be
any dust on the knobby sculpture?

The day
is as self-contained
as the life of a stylite—
pure as "Persimmons"
by Mu-ch'i.

Step
out and the sidewalks crack.
Brisk willows
don't budge in the snow.

Stone
sober this morning
I can't bear the thought
of deliberate action—not

with the world
so shined by the weather.

BEFORE THE STORM

One summer, high in Wyoming
we drove nine miles and paid
to see the great whale, pickled
and hauled on a flatcar crosscountry.
"Throat no bigger'n a orange,"
the man said, in a smell to high
heaven. I wonder how Jonah
could weather that rubbery household
tangled in fish six fathoms down.
Now, bleached by the sun and
shunted to a siding, the gray
beast lay dissolving in chains.

It was none of my business
late in the day, while overhead
Stars and Stripes Forever played
in a national breeze, to sidle
past ropes and poke with a ginger
finger, nostril and lip and eye
till Hey! said the man, keep away
from my whale! But too late,
too late. I had made my mark.
The eye in its liquid socket swung,
the jaw clanged shut, and all the way home
through the bone-dry gullies I could
hear the heart as big as a bushel
beat. O weeks I went drowned
while red-winged grasshoppers span
like flying fish, and the mile-high
weather gathered its forces.

ELEGIAC

Morning, this morning wakes me
to April, nostalgia, insouciant
season, whose importance
like the ambition of the Romans
is chiefly historical. I
remember Quinn's, where fat Sylvia
tended bar, bleached blond;

the beer was rich, the glasses full
and Spring came staggering up the hill
to light with his riot forsythia,
the flowering plum on 42nd,
and expire in a thirst at the door.
Loggers, householders, a renegade
scholar: *numero deus impare gaudet:*

what a bunch of characters, Quinn
said, very Roman, who one day tired
of dice, music, good fellowship
and gave his name to a fishmarket
in the north end of town, a change
the world widely ignored. O
this morning I think of it sadly.

THE DISTANCE ANYWHERE

My neighbor, a lady from Fu-kien
has rearranged her yard completely.
She has cut down the willow tree,
burning it, piecemeal, against a city
ordinance, and has put in its place
her garden of strange herbs.

I confess I resent the diligence
her side of the fence—the stink
of that oriental spinach she hangs
on the clothesline to dry, and the squawk
of the chicken I suspect she keeps,
against a city ordinance, shut up
in the white garage, eventual soup.

But when, across the rows of what-
ever she grows, she brings her
fabulous speech to bear, birds
in the trees, the very butterflies
unbend, acknowledging, to syllables
of that exacter scale, she'd make
the neighborhood, the unaccustomed
air, for all the world to see,
sight, sound and smell, Fu-kien,
beyond our ordinances, clear.

THE DIVIDE

after Lin Ho-ching

I confess I get moony
when I see these
out of the way places.

Parked for a minute
I look down at
the clapboard houses.

Foot of the hill
I drink spring water
so cold my back teeth ache.

God! childhood!
how soon I forgot it!

MONTANA

after Lin Ho-ching

Just over the border
a handful of stores
both sides of the road—
grocery, filling station, feed store
drug store, depot, tavern.

I wait on the platform
for the one daily train south.
The vapors of summer rise over the rails
and the dust shines, north and south.
From somewhere a black dog
is going home obliquely.

After three months
I still don't much want to leave.
Every day like today—acrid & flat & spare
but with beautiful small signs
as August dies.

Now there's a fat blues
spilling from the door of Ed's Happy Haven
and the neon comes on
(before night does)
seeming to say to me Don't
go   Don't go   Come back

FIRST OF ALL

First of all it is necessary
to find yourself a country
—which is not easy.
It takes much looking
after which you must be lucky.
There must be rocks and water
and a sky that is willing
to take itself for granted
without being overbearing.

There should be fresh fish
in the harbor, fresh bread
in the local stores.
The people should know
how to suffer without
being unhappy, and how to be happy
without feeling guilty. The men
should be named Dimitrios
Costa, John or Evangelos
and all the women should be
named Elena or Anthoula.
The newspapers should always
lie, which gives you something
to think about. There should be
great gods in the background
and on all the mountaintops.
There should be lesser gods
in the fields, and nymphs
about all the cool fountains.
The past should be always
somewhere in the distance,
not taken too seriously
but there always giving perspective.
The present should consist of the seven
days of the week forever.
The music should be broken-hearted
without being self-indulgent.
It should be difficult to sing.
Even the birds in the trees should
work for a dangerous living.
When it rains there should be
no doubt about it. The people
should be hard to govern
and not know how to queue up.

They should come from the villages
and go out to sea, and go back
to the villages. There should be
no word in their language
for self-pity. They should be
farmers and sailors, with only
a few poets. The olive trees
and the orange trees and the cypress
will change your life, the rocks
and the lies and the gods
and the strict music. If you go there
you should be prepared to leave
at a moment's notice, knowing
after all you have been somewhere.

Richard Hugo
(1923-   )

DUWAMISH

Midwestern in the heat, this river's
curves are slow and sick. Water knocks
at mills and concrete plants, and crud
compounds the gray. On the out-tide,
water, half salt water from the sea,
rambles by a barrel of molded nails,
gray lumber piles, moss on ovens
in the brickyard no one owns.
Boys are snapping tom cod spines
and jeering at the Greek who bribes
the river with his sailing coins.

Because the name is Indian, Indians
ignore the river as it cruises
past the tavern. Gulls are diving crazy
where boys nail porgies to the pile.
No Indian would interrupt his beer
to tell the story of the snipe
who dove to steal the nailed girl
late one autumn, with the final salmon in.

This river colors day. On bright days
here, the sun is always setting or obscured
by one cloud. Or the shade extended
to the far bank just before you came.
And what should flare, the Chinese red
of a searun's fin, the futile roses,
unkept cherry trees in spring, is muted.
For the river, there is late November
only, and the color of a slow winter.

On the short days, looking for a word,
knowing the smoke from the small homes
turns me colder than wind from
the cold river, knowing this poverty
is not a lack of money but of friends,
I come here to be cold. Not silver cold
like ice, for ice has glitter. Gray
cold like the river. Cold like 4 P.M.
on Sunday. Cold like a decaying porgy.

But cold is a word. There is no word along
this river I can understand or say.
Not Greek threats to a fishless moon
nor Slavic chants. All words are Indian.
Love is Indian for water, and madness
means, to Redmen, I am going home.

AT THE STILLI'S MOUTH

This river ground to quiet in Sylvana.
Here, the quick birds limp and age
or in flight run out of breath and quit.
Poplars start and then repeat the wind
and wind repeats the dust that cakes the girl
who plays a game of wedding in the road
where cars have never been. The first car
will be red and loaded with wild grooms.

August rain says go to blackmouth,
violate the tin piled derelict against
the barn and glowing like the luck
a fugitive believed until he found
this land too flat for secrets
and the last hill diving on him
like a starved bird. The crude dike,
slag and mud and bending out of sight,
left gray the only color for the sky,
wind the only weather, neo-Holland
printed with no laughter on the map.

That hermit in the trailer at the field's
forgotten corner, he has moments, too—
a perfect solo on a horn he cannot play,
applauding sea, special gifts of violets
and cream. In bed at 5 P.M.
he hears the rocks of children on his roof
threatening his right to waste his life.

With the Stilli this defeated and the sea
turned slough by close Camano, how can water die
with drama, in a final rich cascade,
a suicide, a victim of terrain, a martyr?
Or need it die? Can't the stale sea tunnel,
climb and start the stream again
somewhere in the mountains where the clinks
of trickle on the stones remind the fry
ending is where rain and blackmouth runs begin?

Now the blackmouth run. The Stilli quivers
where it never moved before. Willows
changed to windmills in the spiteless eye.
Listen. Fins are cracking like the wings
of quick birds trailing rivers through the sky.

INDIAN GRAVES AT JOCKO

for Victor Charlo

These dirt mounds make the dead seem fat.
Crude walls of rock that hold the dirt
when rain rides wild, were placed with skill
or luck. No crucifix can make
the drab boards of this chapel Catholic.
A mass across these stones becomes
whatever wail the wind decides is right.

They asked for, got the Black Robe
and the promised masses, well meant
promises, shabby third hand crosses.
This graveyard can expand, can crawl
in all directions to the mountains,
climb the mountains to the salmon
and a sun that toned the arrows
when animals were serious as meat.

The dead are really fat, the houses lean
from lack of loans. The river runs
a thin bed down the useless flat
where Flathead homes are spaced like friends.
The dead are strange
jammed this familial. A cheap fence
separates the chapel from the graves.

A forlorn lot like this, where snow
must crawl to find the tribal stones,
is more than just a grim result of cheat,
Garfield's forgery, some aimless trek
of horses from the stolen Bitter Root.
Dead are buried here because the dead
will always be obscure, wind
the one thing whites will always give a chance.

BEAR PAW

The wind is 95. It still pours from the east
like armies and it drains each day of hope.
From any point on the surrounding rim,
below, the teepees burn. The wind
is infantile and cruel. It cries 'give in' 'give in'
and Looking Glass is dying on the hill.
Pale grass shudders. Cattails beg and bow.
Down the draw, the dust of anxious horses
hides the horses. When it clears, a car
with Indiana plates is speeding to Chinook.

That bewildering autumn, the air howled
garbled information and the howl of coyotes
blurred the border. Then a lull in wind.
V after V of Canada geese. Silence
on the highline. Only the eternal nothing
of space. This is Canada and we are safe.
You can study the plaques, the unique names
of Indians and bland ones of the whites,
or study books, or recreate from any point
on the rim the action. Marked stakes tell you
where they fell. Learn what you can. The wind
takes all you learn away to reservation graves.

If close enough to struggle, to take blood
on your hands, you turn your weeping face
into the senile wind. Looking Glass is dead
and will not die. The hawk that circles overhead
is starved for carrion. One more historian
is on the way, his cloud on the horizon.
Five years from now the wind will be 100,
full of Joseph's words and dusting plaques.
Pray hard to weather, that lone surviving god,
that in some sudden wisdom we surrender.

DRIVING MONTANA

The day is a woman who loves you. Open.
Deer drink close to the road and magpies
spray from your car. Miles from any town
your radio comes in strong, unlikely
Mozart from Belgrade, rock and roll
from Butte. Whatever the next number,
you want to hear it. Never has your Buick
found this forward a gear. Even
the tuna salad in Reedpoint is good.

Towns arrive ahead of imagined schedule.
Absorakee at one. Or arrive so late—
Silesia at nine—you recreate the day.
Where did you stop along the road
and have fun? Was there a runaway horse?
Did you park at that house, the one
alone in a void of grain, white with green
trim and red fence, where you know you lived
once? You remembered the ringing creek,
the soft brown forms of far off bison.
You must have stayed hours, then drove on.
In the motel you know you'd never seen it before.

Tomorrow will open again, the sky wide
as the mouth of a wild girl, friable
clouds you lose yourself to. You are lost
in miles of land without people, without
one fear of being found, in the dash
of rabbits, soar of antelope, swirl
merge and clatter of streams.

Edward Lueders
(1923-   )

RODEO

Leathery, wry, and rough,
Jaw full of chaw, and slits
For eyes—this guy is tough.
He climbs the slatted fence,
Pulls himself atop and sits;
Tilts back his cowboy hat,
Stained with sweat below
The crown, and wipes a dirty
Sleeve across his brow;
Then pulls the hat down tight,
Caresses up its sides,
And spits into the dust
A benediction.

Gracelessly, his Brahma bull
Lunges into the chute
And swings a baleful
Eye around, irresolute.

Vision narrower still,
The man regards the beast.
There's weight enough to kill,
Bone and muscle fit at least
To jar a man apart.
The cowboy sniffs and hitches at
His pants. Himself all heart
And gristle, he watches as
The hands outside the chute
Prepare the sacrificial act.
Standing now, and nerving up,
He takes his final measure
Of the creature's awful back.

Then he moves. Swerving up
And into place, he pricks
The Brahma's bullish pride.

The gate swings free, and
Screams begin to sanctify
Their pitching, tortured ride.

A TOUR OF THE SOUTHWEST

There are no nymphs on deserts,
    where twisted trees, the cacti,
    and the earth itself are male;
    where winds alone distill from dust
    the dryads dreaming there
    and spin them—sudden dervish devils—
    soundlessly, and
    senselessly, and
    aimlessly in air.

Nymphs prefer the sounds of sea,
    the pull, the pound, the suck of surf
    that shapes the sand and sends up spray.
    For nymphs are mist—essential
    moisture that defies evap-
    oration. The shoreline suits them.
    Damp and salt-sweet, they sigh, caress,
    dissolve, and kiss with liquid tongues
    our sensate sands—
    forever re-
    arranging the debris.

THE MAN IN OVERALLS

"That's the end of that,"
the man in overalls
replied. He was tearing
out and raking up
geraniums the heavy snow
had blasted, and I,
having watched those mad
geraniums for months,
had complimented him.

Throughout our easy fall
that tangled plot of his,
that vivid bed
of stubborn flowers,
had held the summer, held
the sun, had held October
a millennium.
          And then
the unexpected snow,
a seal of quiet cold,
had smothered all the growth
and settled things.

So flatly, in reply
to my condolences
and warm appreciation,
and looking not at me
but at the ground which he
was working over, "That's
the end of that," he said,
the man in overalls.

Anthony Ostroff
(1923-   )

IN PUERTO VALLARTA

"Where is the In place . . . ? It is Puerto Vallarta . . ."
—Time, Nov. 1, 1963

Upon a time the jaguars came
Nightly down the hill.
They prowled the town and looked
For human game.
Every door is still
      locked
Where the natives live.
Tomorrow thirty jeeps arrive.
A taxi fleet to move the tourists
And be primitive.

When a jaguar took a child, it is said,
Both screamed.
      Not a sound
Escaped the village.
      Dead
Of night. South, the Olmec God
That killed wore a jaguar mask.
The tourists ask around: What's new?
Who's come to stay? Who sleeps
With whom?
      The sun creeps
Across the waters and goes down.
The all-night light goes on in town.

And from this lisping coast
The Aztecs may have started out
To Mexico. Now breech clout
And gold brassiere
      are surely here.

What's history but fiction?
The cancerous sun, the jaguar
Are time's most dark religion,
But fun to know about.
                              We're all
Well-read. The tourists are
In love with fame
                              and watch for stars.
They swim
At "The Beach of the Dead."

Danger keeps to the hills.
They're building three new hotels
Along the beach.
                              The natives have to sell.
One by one they disappear.
The morning tide still whispers in.
        The rich
Can buy a jaguar skin
For dollars. This is paradise.
Reality is here. Let us
Be true, My Dear.

Prices rise.

ON THE BEACH

I'll write about the world then
sitting here in tropic Mexico
idle as a leaf.

In earth ores, the sun.
Heaven is mother-of-pearl.
Light & color, the foliage burns.

(Elsewhere buildings burn,
newsprint, people burn,
colorless as clear glass.)

The brown-skinned children
opalesce
in the blue delicate surf.

Shrieking innocence
they multiply. Far
great waves are gathering.

LOOKING OUT TO SEA

After a sketch by Clifford Wright

The boardwalk, like a pier, extends
Us upon the blue. The pier is like
A boardwalk, floating as the planet floats,
Serenely in its changing place. You see
Blue space and know piers beneath the pier
Anchor it somewhere, but where you stand
The rough planks are what you stand on. If
The pier's piers float on sand, so
Stars and stellar systems float—grand
Amusement parks on piers. Here we are.
And there, the pier's end. Beyond, the blue
Water, sky—how far, how high, we tell
By that Victorian lady and the boy
With bicycle and pack, the wire angel
That's for dressmakers, placed there, too,
And those two old folk at the very edge—
The brink, you'd almost say. He seems to be
Looking down to see how deep, and she,
Hausfrau, clutches his arm to hold him back.
The boy with the pack, nearer, looks—it seems—
At the young Victorian woman with her hair
Upswept and skirt trailing (billowing,
Maybe) and left hand raised to say "You see!"
As she exclaims the sea or sky—those gay
Distances. And yet it may be
The boy is looking not at her but where
The wonderful sea monster rises there
Just at her side, admonished by her right
Cautionary hand: He's not to interfere

137

With land creatures' looks to sea. He,
The monster, in his awkward coils, is sweet
And quizzical—and forfeits being wet
To be beside his lady, watched by
The gilded, rusting dummy that once held
His lady's dress, perhaps. But she looks out.
Ah! Clouds! Currents of high air,
Of sea, of sun! Such blues! And that cool breeze!
And we see, too, how waters become seas,
And seas horizons, piers planets, gulls
(There are no gulls) and monsters pure angels.
If, from here, you choose looking out to sea,
There's nothing to be seen but summer clarities.

ABOUT LONG DAYS

There are long days and short ones to be told.
The short are easier, both in bearing and
in telling, but how do you describe the long?
Then things do not go by in a rush of sunlight
or love or anticipation: the honest job
that can be done. Winter's short days are long,
for instance—longest in winter rain that comes
coldly into the gray snow. But how
do you describe that length? Isolate
one small thing to be seen? Not the cows
hunched in the cold rain there in the field
of slowly dissolving snow, who morosely chew
at the pile of hay beneath its wet gray lid.
Not the man in the parked pick-up watching them
in the heavy light as the gray-green stream beyond
the road swells with the runoff, threatening flood.
Then that one drop of water caught inside
his truck door window, running its clear trail
crazily down the fogged glass past which
he tries to focus on those cows who blur?

Or the shallow, cold continuous line the rain
and snow melt make around the hooves—say
one forehoof of that one cow there where she
has planted it three inches deep in the pure
black puddle with its wisps of straw that float
beside the drenched hock to which they'll cling
if the water rises, rises fast enough.

THE ZOO

The elephant never forgets.
Africa sailed away,
The forests burned,
And all the streams went dry.
But as his great bulk turns
Within his tiny eye,
As if those wrinkles smiled,
The lowing song is heard.

The polar bear never forgets.
The arctic thawed apart,
The water warmed,
And all the cold fish died.
But as he roars alarm
And turns within his cage
His huge paws form
Their great, applauding heart.

Even the turtledove
Whose sky has lost its air
Does not forget,
And from his wire bar,
Perched for that old wit
Of green and sun, stares out
On flying doves, and yet
Sings yet again of love.

Emma Lou Thayne
(1924-   )

THE BLUE TATTOO

(On hearing of an offer by the medical school to pay $1,000 cash for claim on any body)

A thousand dollars now (cash).
And who'd know but me? And maybe whoever
keeps the record or does the tattoos.
A thousand dollars now, cash.

A little blue tattoo on my right big toe
saying I'm theirs, no matter when I die.
What difference would it make when I'm dead?
Who ever thinks of bodies anyhow, in graves—or labs?

    Dr. Kiwamoto took us in Anatomy One
    past the door with black letters "Medical
    Students Only" (The Gross lab). He understood
    how boring plastic (all parts removable) models
    and pickled putty-colored embryos could get.
    (He laughed a lot.)

I wonder if they'd let me buy me back, maybe
with interest. Sometime when a thousand dollars
wouldn't mean a thing.

    The rich formaldahyde, the wrinkled sheet,
    the swoop that bared the gray green (like
    Kindergarten clay) cadaver.

How awful would the wondering become? How urgent
not to die? How careful would I be, tattooed with
brittle fear? I could fool them all. And chop
or blow my toe off. And only limp. Or have a
plastic surgeon sand the blue away.

Sliced smooth from sternum to groin
the stubbled (they say they grow hair and
fingernails after they die) man lay parted
like Grand Canyon, one side cavernous
beside the severed cliff impressed
with fossils and striations of what
used to work. And neatly along the hollow
(clean but green) a lined-up liver, lung,
spleen, intestine, and (How lucky he'd not
had it out!) appendix scalpeled smooth
for an A in Gross.

A thousand dollars now, cash.
I'm not my body, flesh, a pound of nothing,
parts assembled to be manipulated by me (in essence).

"He's Pierre." The doctor smiling, flinging
the smell across the dead (dead) man. "Some
guys get so used to this they eat their lunch
while they carve."

You can get up to five-hundred dollars just for
your eyes. And what's the price for flying
into myself intact, Sistine fingers reaching (almost),
my God?

SHOT

Now, Morphine, now. Blend
    with the sheets.
Flatten feeling like
    a hose on dust.
Spread me liquid along
    the shudder where
my legs have been. Melt
    my hips. Flood
the ragged heaviness
    along my back.
Fizz it out my
    airy palms. Now
my head. Swamp
    the squirming. Let
it drown. Then if
    it dries, curl it
up to roll away
    and corner sleep.

No. Don't slither
    off in trails of
me. Don't wisp away
    like fumes at inter-
sections. Don't lump
    me here on this
fierce bed to wait.

MANCHILD

A snowmobile:
Helicopter skeleton innocuous
on forelegs of flattened metal
and corrugated belly!
I've never tried one.
Skis yes.
The icy drop
alone.

But now a lanky boy
to drive.
Why not?
So on behind his easy arrogance.

Off the safe plateau
and into fluff
on top of thirteen feet packed
firmly into March. Our creature
leaps and shies but clings
to curling edges of ravines,
its pulse and power controlled
by shifting parka shoulders.
It leans at awful angles which,
if tipped one icy breath to left
or right, will roll us
into almost tempting crypts
an age below.

I hang on. Arms full,
knees gripping leather flesh,
eyes pinched against
our own fierce wind,
elbows aching, hair
shocked out,
and laugh.
Unable not to laugh
with frozen teeth
the laugh of giddy fear.
I feel the cocky
confidence that steers
our lonely cone of noise,
and with my laugh blown white
into an unfeigned wintry
moment, wonder
how would it be
to have a boy?

John Haines
(1924-   )

LEAVES AND ASHES

Standing where the city and the forest
were walled together,
she dreamed intently on a stone.

A passage cut in its granite face
told of the sea at morning,
how a hand grew steady in its depth.

Then a cold wind blew through the oaks;
the leaves at her feet got up
like startled children, whirled
and fled along the wintry ground.
In the soil a jar of ashes
settled and slept.

It was at the end of a steep
and bitter decade, in a year of burials,
of houses sold, the life they held
given away for the darkness to keep.

She stood alone in the windy arbor,
the tall brown house of November
slowly unbuilding around her.

THE WEAVER

for Blair

By a window in the west
where the orange light falls,
a girl sits weaving in silence.

She picks up threads of sunlight,
thin strands from the blind shadows
fallen to the floor,
as her slim hands swiftly pass
through the cords of her loom.

Light from a wine glass
goes into the weave,
light passing from the faces
of those who watch her;
now the grey flash from a mirror
darkening against the wall.

And her batten comes down,
softly beating the threads,
a sound that goes and comes again,
weaving this house and the dusk
into one seamless, deepening cloth.

THE CALENDAR

Let this book as it ends
remember the hand that wrote it,
the eye that slowly
learned its alphabet,
the thumb that peeled back its pages.

The days were marked beforehand:
phases of the moon,
a flight to Pennsylvania,
the changing birthdays of children.

Words, cyphers on paper,
paper that curls and yellows,
Valentines, Easters,
a lot of numbers to throw away . . .

Something about a year
dying in anger,
something about starlight and sleep.

Robin Skelton
(1925-   )

HISTORY

i. m. J.F.K.

I am a monster.
Among small
crouching years,
I take up

Death in my hand
and Death shakes
wild as a shrew.
I pile bones

high by the wall.
I eat graves.
Chanting,
they bring me
graves to eat.

LETTER V

Between us quiet has fallen.
The space of air
silvered with sea-mist hangs
like a waiting bird
between the west and the east
of sun and sun,
alien to birth or closure,
our one day
perpetually transfigurings of light.

Creation builds no mountains here,
no beast
bears rhythmed hair and blood
through the stiff air,
and no past has reflected
on white stones
a scratched chronology
of kings and spells.
For this is not of time,
nor yet of place
caught in its green beginnings,
but the poise
of that one thought
which is before and after
and out of which
perpetually the waves
of universes, worlds,
and seemings move
to bring the voyage
underneath this sky.
And now, my dear, we wait,
if this is waiting
which has dissolved all time
and cannot end,
but only out of its white space construct
the acts and images we must employ
to keep us steady here,
where balance dies,
and we ask no recalling.
And we wait,
not for, but in, our being;
no until
pledges our minds to longing,
for we are
the always of ourselves,
and love, like mist,
encloses with its silver
endless seas.

THE GIFT

I would send you
a rose, golden
and flared wide,
but there's no rose
wide and golden
enough to spell
out the sunlight
that I would send.

I would send you
a prayer, but all
those words are wooden;
their hasps rust:
I would send you
a ring, but rings
are meant for lovers,
and we are less.

Therefore I send
not rose, prayer, ring,
but this which brings
what I would send.

THE TWO SLEEPERS

Alone in her bed,
red hair outspread,
sea-sounds beyond the door,
the brown roof-beams
protect the dreams
that tread the brown wood floor

and whisper, whisper
through the night
their shiverings of wings,
while I, by cross
and candle-light,
think on the three last things.

Ralph Salisbury
(1926-   )

IN THE CHILDREN'S MUSEUM IN NASHVILLE

In the Children's Museum in Nashville, rattlesnakes coil,
protected by glass and by placards warning that if teased
they might just dash their brains against apparent air.
Negroes are advised that, if notified in advance,
the Children's Museum in Nashville will take care of them
on certain days. On an uncertain day, to regulate
my sons by Mother Nature's whims, I make it quite clear
that some skulls are less substantial than apparent air,
as, evidently, one empty cage verifies.
More durable are the heads of bison, eland
(from Africa) and other exhibits: a purple parrot,
who, eventually, condescends to demonstrate,
by winking, that, far from dead, he of his own free will
dreams over caged snakes in his own cage; blades
from China's dynasties and Malayan tribes;
some shrunken Jivaro noggins and a diminished Nashville;
and, most awesome, a bird and a squirrel
reborn at intervals from blacked-out flesh as white
skeletons. On Sundays, children are allowed a look
at electric stars. Seen every day is an Indian
child—cured by chance, the signs say,
in a dry, airless place—still possessed
of parchment skin, though eyeless, and still dressed
in ceremonial regalia
that celebrates his remove to a better world.

A HALO

In somebody's shoes   some Gypsies war-dance water to their Roman tower
Moors wrecked   and clouds   sifting   like flour over Friday fish
Down from the Malaga hills   become the smoke of Great Grandad's
Stockade   sunset in it   a halo   pink

Gibraltar pales   to my father's pipe-puff   drifting above the white
Capped waves of uncut Christmas trees   the day the blood of a fox
Made snow seem sunset surf

More vivid than fur   chicken-fat sleeked   a halo of red widened
Pink turning red and a further pink appearing   as air   which haiku
Had shaped   is said to have spread from Hiroshima   and still—
As a home smashed bones of Romans moulder under   genes in the marrow
Powdered asunder   an asteroid belt   of babies—   still as stone
Again dims   pink spreads from red spreading from red   and spreads
And spreads   against the dark

UNDER THE CELLAR

Roman ruins below
bomb-rubble in London, I
try to tumble from
my second-story study to what is
under the storm-cellar my father, himself
a tornado when drunk,
sober, thundered his brood to shelter in
and perched, alone
at the top of the stairs, all dark
those moments the earth became all
flame, the time
Dad saw and I only felt
the Blitzkrieg of Londinium on the Thames
on our Iowa farm, the time
so many huge things took wing.

WINTER 1970, FOX RIVER, ILLINOIS

Gone south, the ice the size of the oven door
raft for bubbles of maybe dreaming catfish,
mirror for snow clouds, may,
in a day, melt like a meteor reaching the atmosphere.
Over the railroad tie that used to be
important to a tree, a levee-piling now, berries
crimson as coals in a gust hang,
stems plunged through new snow,
as are my legs, reaching, as far
as surfaces—those of their roots, that are their mouths,
and those of strata of clay, and those
of my feet and boots—reaching as far
as surfaces will let them reach
toward the center of an earth said
to be round as a berry or
the bubble of a dreaming catfish.

David Wagoner
(1926-   )

THE SINGING LESSON

You must stand erect but at your ease, a posture
Demanding a compromise
Between your spine and your head, your best face forward,
Your willful hands
Not beckoning or clenching or sweeping upward
But drawn in close:
A man with his arms spread wide is asking for it,
A martyred beggar,
A flightless bird on the nest dreaming of flying.
For your full resonance
You must keep your inspiring and expiring moments
Divided but equal,
Not locked like antagonists from breast to throat
Choking toward silence.

If you have learned, with labor and luck, the measures
You were meant to complete,
You may find yourself before an audience
Singing into the light,
Transforming the air you breathe—that malleable wreckage,
That graveyard of shouts,
That inexhaustible pool of chatter and whimpers—
Into deathless music.
But remember, with your mouth wide open, eyes shut,
Some men will wonder,
When they look at you without listening, whether
You're singing or dying.
Take care to be heard. But even singing alone,
Singing for nothing,
Singing to empty space in no one's honor,
Keep time: it will tell
When you must give the final end-stopped movement
Your tacit approval.

THE LABORS OF THOR

Stiff as the icicles in their beards, the Ice Kings
Sat in the great cold hall and stared at Thor
Who had lumbered this far north to stagger them
With his gifts, which (back at home) seemed scarcely human.

"Immodesty forbids," his sideman Loki
Proclaimed throughout the preliminary bragging
And reeled off Thor's accomplishments, fit for Sagas
Or a seat on the bench of the gods. With a sliver of beard

An Ice King picked his teeth: "Is he a drinker?"
And Loki boasted of challengers laid out
As cold as pickled herring. The Ice King offered
A horn-cup long as a harp's neck, full of mead.

Thor braced himself for elbow and belly room
And tipped the cup and drank as deep as mackerel,
Then deeper, reaching down for the halibut
Till his broad belt buckled. He had quaffed one inch.

"Maybe he's better at something else," an Ice King
Muttered, yawning. Remembering the boulders
He'd seen Thor heave and toss in the pitch of anger,
Loki proposed a bout of lifting weights.

"You men have been humping rocks from here to there
For ages," an Ice King said. "They cut no ice.
Lift something harder." And he whistled out
A gray-green cat with cold, mouseholey eyes.

Thor gave it a pat, then thrust both heavy hands
Under it, stooped and heisted, heisted again,
Turned red in the face and bit his lip and heisted
From the bottom of his heart—and lifted one limp forepaw.

Now pink in the face himself, Loki said quickly
That heroes can have bad days, like bards and beggars,
But Thor of all mortals was the grossest wrestler
And would stake his demigodhood on one fall.

Seeming too bored to bother, an Ice King waved
His chilly fingers around the mead-hall, saying,
"Does anyone need some trifling exercise
Before we go glacier-calving in the morning?"

An old crone hobbled in, foul-faced and gamy,
As bent in the back as any bitch of burden,
As gray as water, as feeble as an oyster.
An Ice King said, "She's thrown some boys in her time."

Thor would have left, insulted, but Loki whispered,
"When the word gets south, she'll be at least an ogress."
Thor reached out sullenly and grabbed her elbow,
But she quicksilvered him and grinned her gums.

Thor tried his patented hammerlock takedown,
But she melted away like steam from a leaky sauna.
He tried a whole Nelson: it shrank to half, to a quarter,
Then nothing. He stood there, panting at the ceiling,

"Who got me into this demigoddiness?"
As flashy as lightning, the woman belted him
With her bony fist and boomed him to one knee,
But fell to a knee herself, as pale as moonlight.

Bawling for shame, Thor left by the back door,
Refusing to be consoled by Loki's plans
For a quick revision of the Northodox Version
Of the evening's deeds, including Thor's translation

From vulnerable flesh and sinew into a dish
Fit for the gods and a full apotheosis
With catches and special effects by the sharpest gleemen
Available in an otherwise flat season.

He went back south, tasting his bitter lesson
Moment by moment for the rest of his life,
Believing himself a pushover faking greatness
Along a tawdry strain of misadventures.

Meanwhile, the Ice Kings trembled in their chairs
But not from the cold: they'd seen a man hoist high
The Great Horn-Cup that ends deep in the ocean
And lower all Seven Seas by his own stature;

They'd seen him budge the Cat of the World and heft
The pillar of one paw, the whole north corner;
They'd seen a mere man wrestle with Death herself
And match her knee for knee, grunting like thunder.

THE MAN WHO SPILLED LIGHT

The man who spilled light wasn't to blame for it.
He was in a hurry to bring it home to the city
Where, everyone said, there was too much darkness:
"Look at those shadows," they said. "They're dangerous.
Who's there? What's that?" and crouching, "Who are *you*?"
So he went and scraped up all the light he could find.

But it was too much to handle and started spilling:
Flakes and star-marks, shafts of it splitting
To ring-light and light gone slack or jagged,
Clouds folded inside out, whole pools
And hummocks and domes of light,
Egg-light, light tied in knots or peeled in swatches,
Daylight as jumbled as jackstraws falling.

Then everything seemed perfectly obvious
Wherever they looked. There was nothing they couldn't see.
The corners and alleys all looked empty,
And no one could think of anything terrible
Except behind their backs, so they all lined up
With their backs to walls and felt perfectly fine.
And the man who'd spilled it felt fine for a while,
But then he noticed people squinting.

They should have been looking at everything, and everything
Should have been perfectly clear, and everyone
Should have seemed perfectly brilliant, there was so much
Dazzle: people were dazzled, they were dazzling,
But they were squinting, trying to make darkness
All over again in the cracks between their eyelids.
So he swept up all the broken light
For pity's sake and put it back where it came from.

SLEEPING IN THE WOODS

Not having found your way out of the woods, begin
Looking for somewhere to bed down at nightfall
Though you have nothing
But parts of yourself to lie on, nothing but skin and backbone
And the bare ungiving ground to reconcile.
From standing to kneeling,
From crouching to turning over old leaves, to going under,
You must help yourself like any animal
To enter the charmed circle
Of the night with a body not meant for stretching or sprawling:
One ear-flap at a time knuckling your skull,
Your stiff neck (needing
An owl's twist to stay even) cross-purposing your spine,
With rigid ankles, with nowhere to put your arms.
But now, lying still
At last, you may watch the shadows seeking their own level,
The ground beneath you neither rising nor falling,
Neither giving nor taking
From the dissolving cadence of your heart, identical darkness
Behind and before your eyes—and you are going
To sleep without a ceiling,
For the first time without walls, not *falling* asleep, not losing
Anything under you to the imponderable
Dead and living
Earth, your countervailing bed, but settling down
Beside it across the slackening threshold
Of the place where it is always
Light, at the beginning of dreams, where the stars, shut out

By leaves and branches in another forest, burn
At the mattering source
Forever, though a dream may have its snout half sunk in blood
And the mind's tooth gnaw all night at bone and tendon
Among the trembling snares:
Whoever stumbles across you in the dark may borrow
Your hidebound substance for the encouragement
Of mites or angels;
But whatever they can't keep is yours for the asking. Turn up
In time, at the first faint stretch of dawn, and you'll see
A world pale-green as hazel,
The chalk-green convolute lichen by your hand like sea fog,
The fallen tree beside you in half-light
Dreaming a greener sapling,
The dead twigs turning over, and your cupped hand lying open
Beyond you in the morning like a flower.
Making light of it,
You have forgotten why you came, have served your purpose, and simply
By being here have found the right way out.
Now, you may waken.

THE LESSON

That promising morning
Driving beside the river,
I saw twin newborn lambs
Still in a daze
At the grassy sunlight;
Beyond them, a day-old colt
As light-hoofed as the mare
That swayed over his muzzle—
Three staggering new lives
Above the fingerlings
From a thousand salmon nests—
And I sang on the logging road
Uphill for miles, then came
To a fresh two thousand acres
Of a familiar forest
Clear-cut and left for dead
By sawtoothed Weyerhaeuser.

157

I haunted those gray ruins
For hours, listening to nothing,
Being haunted in return
By vacancy, vacancy,
Till I grew as gray as stumps
Cut down to size. They drove me
Uphill, steeper and steeper,
Thinking: the salmon will die
In gillnets and crude oil,
The colt be broken and broken,
And the lambs leap to their slaughter.

I found myself in a rage
Two-thirds up Haystack Mountain
Being buzzed and ricochetted
By a metallic whir
That jerked me back toward life
Among young firs and cedars—
By a rufous hummingbird
Exulting in wild dives
For a mate perched out of sight
And cackling over and over,
Making me crouch and cringe
In his fiery honor.

THE LOST STREET

*"Just imagine: tomorrow morning you get in your car to go to work. You
start to pull out of the driveway, but—no street."*
—What Highways Mean to You,
Auto Dealers Traffic Safety Council

You sit for a moment, idling, remembering
Another street running away from you
Before you learned to walk
Across it, even beside it: strange as a river
Under the elmtrees, it blurred
Uphill as far as the hospital
Or downhill into the dark city.

158

But this one, no longer stretching toward work,
Had been different, indifferent,
As easy to forget as a hall carpet
Leading from sleep to worry, from love
To bewilderment, from the steep hillside
Up to the greenhouse and the reservoir
Or down to the dimmed-out, burning city.

Now the deepening grass and brambles
Remind you there was somewhere you were going
Around the house instead of looking through glass
At this barely believable morning: you must get out
Of the car and stand on the ground,
Then kneel on it like a penitent gardener,
Touching it with your hands, crawling again to know it.

THE DEATH AND RESURRECTION OF THE BIRDS

Falling asleep, the birds are falling
Down through the last light's thatchwork farther than rain,
Their grace notes dwindling
Into that downy pit where the first bird
Waits to become them in the nest of the night.

Silent and featherless,
Now they are one dark bird in darkness.

Beginning again, the birds are breaking
Upward, new-fledged at daybreak, their clapping wingbeats
Striking the sides of the sun, the singing brilliant
Dust spun loose on the wind from the end to the beginning.

TALKING BACK

This green-and-red, yellow-naped Amazon parrot, Pythagoras,
Is the master of our kitchen table. *Every good boy*
Does fine! he shouts, hanging upside down, and *Pieces of eight*
And gold doubloons! in his cage whose latches he picked with ease
Till we bought a padlock, *To market, to market, to buy a fat pig!*
Home again, home again, and he rings his brass bell, as militant
As salvation, or knocks his trapeze like a punching bag with his beak
Or outfakes and ripostes the treacherous cluster of measuring spoons
Which he pretends are out for his blood. How many times
Have I wished him back in his jungle? Instead, he brings it here
Daily with a voice like sawgrass in raucous counterpoint
To after-work traffic, washing machines, or electric razors
As he jangles back at motors in general, *Who knows*
What evil lurks in the hearts of men? but then, inscrutably,

Refusing to laugh like The Shadow. When he walks on the table
In a fantailed pigeon-toed shuffling strut, getting a taste
Of formica with his leathery tongue, he challenges me
Each morning to fight for my wife if I dare to come near her,
Ruffling his neck and hunching, beak open, his amber eyes
Contracting to malevolent points. I taught him everything
He knows, practically, *Fair and foul are near of kin!*
Including how to love her as he croons in her soft voice,
I'm a green bird, and how to test me for the dialectic hell of it,
What then? sang Plato's ghost, What then? as if I knew
The answer which Yeats in his finite wisdom forgot to teach me.

Keith Wilson
(1927-   )

THE MORNING OF THE WOLF

The first time I saw him, he rose
out of the grass of a hill, his eyes
straight into mine, big head low

He moved toward me, ignoring the man
who stood beside me with the gun, his eyes
straight into mine. I was thirteen,
taught to hate and fear wolves. He, a *lobo,*
a Mexican wolf from below the border.
His eyes. I keep coming back to that.
The way they bore the center of me.

The gun began firing, wildly, bullets
splashing dust around the wolf but he
barely moved, his eyes never left mine
until I broke the contact and saw the man
his hands shaking, spraying the .22 bullets,
caught completely in "buck fever," the wolf
almost laughing, eased off through the grass
his tail a contemptous banner
—his every movement sure of the morning, me,
the long years I would remember his yellow eyes
that big head looking at me.

I recall the smell of sage
and creosote, the fear of that man, courage
of the wolf. Held in my brain, he never
went away at all. His footsteps sound outside
my city window; his cry rises and falls
on the dawn wind.

DAY OF THE WOLF

The other ranchers came this morning,
early; in the crisp blue air of Fall
they stood stiffly—each holding his reins
his restless horse, took coffee, nodding
a "thank-you-man," his rifle hanging
beside him in a scratched leather
scabbard.

       —the wolf was back, three calves
slaughtered yesterday, their white faces flat
on the ground, big eyes splattered with dirt

Wolf, running free past the traps in search
of fresh meat, he couldn't be fooled by bait.

That evening we got him just the same,
shot him down when he came to smell
the bitch coyote we'd staked out,
got him, horses in a circle he
couldn't cross, but he fought well,
stood his ground, slugs slapping
him down, him getting up, snarling
showing his teeth until he died.

The horses wouldn't carry his hide
back and we left it there, bloody in the
dusk, his skinny body white as a child's
in the waving tall grass.

COYOTES FIGHTING

—from a woodcut by George Vlahos

Turning, orange and black, dream
crimson

      teeth white with moonlight

the blood more an illusion than
a part of their own curiously fierce
laughter

      even the fight
a joke for bitches, showoffs, bluffing
the night and its clear stars, *coyotes*
on a ricepaper background, fragile
as the soft pads of their feet, circling.

OLD TOBY

Riding down the hillroad in his red pickup,
thinking of him, how he died, bullet from the gun
I gave him, the spun & tangled web of his life.

My own life, caught briefly glistening in the sticky
threads, what he had meant, come to be—a friend, all
the touches, moments contained therein:

      & quite suddenly there he
was, leaning into the shadow of the pickup's cab,
an old familiar look in his eye. "Toby!" I shouted,
"Wow, man, I thought you were dead!" So glad to see
him, above all men, he had come back from wherever
they took him, he was *back.*

                    He didn't say anything,
smoke curling upward, the panel lights gleaming
on his smooth face. Then he turned, I saw his
bulletshattered cheek; the other half, twin wreckage
of the first, the missing eye was a bloody hole
as he reached, gurgling deep in his chest for
the steering wheel & the pickup headed for the canyon,
headlights groping for the dark

                    I fought back,
knowing from the unholy light of that one eye
what it was I fought, his blood all over me,
his cold hand against mine the night spun out past
the stars to a place where all the webs are blackness,
all friends merely companions in horror.

Philip Levine
(1928-   )

A NEW DAY

The headlights fading out at dawn,
A stranger at the shore, the shore
Not wakening to the great sea
Out of sleep, and night, and no sun
Rising where it rose before.

The old champion in a sweat suit
Tells me this is Chicago, this—
He does not say—is not the sea
But the chopped grey lake you get to
After travelling all night

From Dubuque, Cairo, or Wyandotte.
He takes off at a slow trot
And the fat slides under his shirt.
I recall the Friday night
In a beer garden in Detroit

I saw him flatten Ezzard Charles
On TV, and weep, and raise
Both gloved hands in a slow salute
To a God. I could tell him that.
I could tell him that those good days

Were no more and no less than these.
I could tell him that I thought
By now I must have reached the sea
We read about, or that last night
I saw a man break down and cry

Out of luck and out of gas
In Bruce's Crossing. We collect
Here at the shore, the two of us,
To make a pact, a people come
For a new world and a new home

And what we get is what we bring:
A grey light coming on at dawn,
No fresh start and no bird song
And no sea and no shore
That someone hasn't seen before.

CLOUDS

I
Dawn. First light tearing
at the rough tongues of the zinnias,
at the leaves of the just born.

Today it will rain. On the road
black cars are abandoned, but the clouds
ride above, their wisdom intact.

They are predictions. They never matter.
The jet fighters lift above the flat roofs,
black arrowheads trailing their future.

II
When the night comes small fires go out.
Blood runs to the heart and finds it locked.

Morning is exhaustion, tranquilizers, gasoline,
the screaming of frozen bearings,
the failures of will, the tv talking to itself.

The clouds go on eating oil, cigars,
housewives, sighing letters,
the breath of lies. In their great silent pockets
they carry off all our dead.

III
The clouds collect until there's no sky.
A boat slips its moorings and drifts
toward the open sea, turning and turning.

The moon bends to the canal and bathes
her torn lips, and the earth goes on
giving off her angers and sighs

and who knows or cares except these
breathing the first rains,
the last rivers running over iron.

IV
You cut an apple in two pieces
and ate them both. In the rain
the door knocked and you dreamed it.
On bad roads the poor walked under cardboard boxes.

The houses are angry because they're watched.
A soldier wants to talk with God
but his mouth fills with lost tags.

The clouds have seen it all, in the dark
they pass over the graves of the forgotten
and they don't cry or whisper.

They should be punished every morning,
they should be bitten and boiled like spoons.

DETROIT GREASE SHOP POEM

Four bright steel crosses,
universal joints, plucked
out of the burlap sack—
"the heart of the drive train"—
the book says. Stars
on Lemon's wooden palm,
stars that must be capped,
rolled, and anointed,
that have their orders
and their commands as he
has his.

Under the blue
hesitant light another day
at Automotive
in the city of dreams.
We're all there to count
and be counted, Lemon,
Rosie, Eugene, Luis,
and me, too young to know
this is for keeps, pinning
on my apron, rolling up
my sleeves.
                    The roof leaks
from yesterday's rain,
the waters gather above us
waiting for one mistake.
When a drop falls on Lemon's
corded arm, he looks at it
as though it were something
rare or mysterious
like a drop of water or
a single lucid meteor
fallen slowly from
nowhere and burning on
his skin like a tear.

BREATH

Who hears the humming
of rocks at great height,
the long steady drone
of granite holding together,
the strumming of obsidian
to itself? I go among
the rocks stooping
and pecking like a
sparrow, imagining
the glacier's final push
resounding still. In
a freezing mountain
stream, my hand opens
scratched and raw and

flutters strangely,
more like an animal
or wild blossom in wind
than any part of me. Great
fields of stone
stretching away under
a slate sky, their single
flower the flower
of my right hand.

                      Last night
the fire died into itself
black stick by stick
and the dark came out
of my eyes flooding
everything. I
slept alone and dreamed
of you in an old house
back home among
your country people,
among the dead, not
any living one besides
yourself. I woke
scared by the gasping
of a wild one, scared
by my own breath, and
slowly calmed
remembering your weight
beside me all these
years, and here and
there an eye of stone
gleamed with the warm light
of an absent star.

                      Today
in this high clear room
of the world, I squat
to the life of rocks
jewelled in the stream
or whispering
like shards. What fears
are still held locked
in the veins till the last

fire, and who will calm
us then under a gold sky
that will be all of earth.
Two miles below on the burning
summer plains, you go
about your life one
more day. I give you
almond blossoms
for your hair, your hair
that will be white, I give
the world my worn-out breath
on an old tune, I give
it all I have
and take it back again.

John S. Harris
(1929-   )

HAY DERRICK

You can see the derrick there
In the lower meadow by the marsh
Where there's a low stack
Of hay against the pale sky.

The father made them unhook the chain
That linked the pole to base
And lowered the end
To rest upon the ground.

But the big pine pole
Used to point toward the sun like a dial
And swing across the summer sky
To raise the loads of meadow hay

That creaking wagons brought to stack—
The Jackson hanging from the block,
With four curved tines like blades of scythes
Dropping down and sinking in the load,

Then hoisting high with cable taut,
Turning slowly in the air,
And swinging over the stack
With the screek of straining blocks—

Then the shout of *yo* to pull
The trip rope and dump the hay,
Returning then to the wagon—
Eight forkfuls for the load.

So they were that August day,
The father pushing the fork into the load,
His son carefully building the stack,
And a child on the plodding derrick horse

That drew the cable up
Then backed to let it down,
In easy rhythm of lower
And hoist and swing and drop.

Then there came a shift of wind
That made the derrick horse start.
The child tried to pull the reins,
But the horse bolted fast.

The empty fork flew to the block
But stopped and then plunged down
Where one tine pinned the son to the stack
And the broken cable covered him with coils.

They left the stack unfinished
To bleach in the summer sun,
And the autumn winds stirred the hay
Like unkempt hair on the head of a boy.

TAG, I.D.

Bright oval on a light chain,
Last name first,
Then Christian name
And middle initial
A number assigned by his master,
A letter for his blood,
Another for his god
Tooth-notched
Stainless steel coin
For the boatman.

Thom Gunn
(1929-   )

IN SANTA MARIA DEL POPOLO

Waiting for when the sun an hour or less
Conveniently oblique makes visible
The painting on one wall of this recess
By Caravaggio, of the Roman School,
I see how shadow in the painting brims
With a real shadow, drowning all shapes out
But a dim horse's haunch and various limbs,
Until the very subject is in doubt.

But evening gives the act, beneath the horse
And one indifferent groom, I see him sprawl,
Foreshortened from the head, with hidden face,
Where he has fallen, Saul becoming Paul.
O wily painter, limiting the scene
From a cacophony of dusty forms
To the one convulsion, what is it you mean
In that wide gesture of the lifting arms?

No Ananias croons a mystery yet,
Casting the pain out under name of sin.
The painter saw what was, an alternate
Candor and secrecy inside the skin.
He painted, elsewhere, that firm insolent
Young whore in Venus' clothes, those pudgy cheats,
Those sharpers; and was strangled, as things went,
For money, by one such picked off the streets.

I turn, hardly enlightened, from the chapel
To the dim interior of the church instead,
In which there kneel already several people,
Mostly old women: each head closeted
In tiny fists holds comfort as it can.
Their poor arms are too tired for more than this
—For the large gesture of solitary man,
Resisting, by embracing, nothingness.

CONSIDERING THE SNAIL

The snail pushes through a green
night, for the grass is heavy
with water and meets over
the bright path he makes, where rain
has darkened the earth's dark. He
moves in a wood of desire,

pale antlers barely stirring
as he hunts. I cannot tell
what power is at work, drenched there
with purpose, knowing nothing.
What is a snail's fury? All
I think is that if later

I parted the blades above
the tunnel and saw the thin
trail of broken white across
litter, I would never have
imagined the slow passion
to that deliberate progress.

Gary Snyder
(1930-   )

MID-AUGUST AT SOURDOUGH
MOUNTAIN LOOKOUT

Down valley a smoke haze
Three days heat, after five days rain
Pitch glows on the fir-cones
Across rocks and meadows
Swarms of new flies.

I cannot remember things I once read
A few friends, but they are in cities.
Drinking cold snow-water from a tin cup
Looking down for miles
Through high still air.

PIUTE CREEK

One granite ridge
A tree, would be enough
Or even a rock, a small creek,
A bark shred in a pool.
Hill beyond hill, folded and twisted
Tough trees crammed
In thin stone fractures
A huge moon on it all, is too much.
The mind wanders. A million
Summers, night air still and the rocks
Warm. Sky over endless mountains.
All the junk that goes with being human
Drops away, hard rock wavers
Even the heavy present seems to fail
This bubble of a heart.
Words and books
Like a small creek off a high ledge
Gone in the dry air.

A clear, attentive mind
Has no meaning but that
Which sees is truly seen.
No one loves rock, yet we are here.
Night chills. A flick
In the moonlight
Slips into Juniper shadow:
Back there unseen
Cold proud eyes
Of Cougar or Coyote
Watch me rise and go.

NOOKSACK VALLEY

February 1956

At the far end of a trip north
In a berry-pickers cabin
At the edge of a wide muddy field
Stretching to the woods and cloudy mountains,
Feeding the stove all afternoon with cedar,
Watching the dark sky darken, a heron flap by,
A huge setter pup nap on the dusty cot.
High rotten stumps in the second-growth woods
Flat scattered farms in the bends of the Nooksack
River. Steelhead run now
   a week and I go back
Down 99, through towns, to San Francisco and Japan.
All America south and east,
Twenty-five years in it brought to a trip-stop
Mind-point, where I turn
Caught more on this land—rock tree and man,
Awake, than ever before, yet ready to leave.
    damned memories,
Whole wasted theories, failures and worse success,
Schools, girls, deals, try to get in
To make this poem a froth, a pity,
A dead fiddle for lost good jobs.
    the cedar walls

Smell of our farm-house, half built in '35.
Clouds sink down the hills
Coffee is hot again. The dog
Turns and turns about, stops and sleeps.

THE LATE SNOW & LUMBER STRIKE
OF THE SUMMER OF FIFTY-FOUR

Whole towns shut down
      hitching the Coast road, only gypos
Running their beat trucks, no logs on
Gave me rides. Loggers all gone fishing
Chainsaws in a pool of cold oil
On back porches of ten thousand
Split-shake houses, quiet in summer rain.
Hitched north all of Washington
Crossing and re-crossing the passes
Blown like dust, no place to work.

Climbing the steep ridge below Shuksan
      clumps of pine
        float out the fog
No place to think or work
      drifting.

On Mt. Baker, alone
In a gully of blazing snow:
Cities down the long valleys west
Thinking of work, but here,
Burning in sun-glare
Below a wet cliff, above a frozen lake,
The whole Northwest on strike
Black burners cold,
The green-chain still,
I must turn and go back:
      caught on a snowpeak
      between heaven and earth
And stand in lines in Seattle.
Looking for work.

Richard Shelton
(1933-   )

TODAY

walked in the front
door and out the back, going
somewhere important,
while the mountains still waited
to be fed and the water
made thousands of sudden decisions.

Now the moon reaches
under the curtain with its tongue.
Wild camels run
through the desert. This is
the floor of the sea
many years later, the breakdown
of organized contemplation.

In a different empire
petty kings would be inspecting
ranks of thumbs at attention
and slaves would be chanting
for miracles in leather,
but we cannot afford mice. Even
spiders visit us rarely
and hurry away to more
comfortable quarters.

I see now that we have
made a success of our failures
and when tomorrow arrives
I will set the dogs on it.

HE WHO REMAINS

you have so much to give they said
so I gave it now it is gone

I stand with my back to a cliff
where stones lean over
looking down at me they are smooth
they have dragged themselves
a long way to get here

years ago I wrote love letters
to distant water and wore
the desire to travel like a hair-shirt

but that is over and regret
was never a friend of mine so I
let him go in search of the others

who departed wearing accidental lives
mocking me calling me *he who remains*

and I remain in the desert
caught in the ropes of myself like
rosaries staying here with penitent
stars whose confessions frighten me

there is no explanation for lights
which move about inside the mountains
and coyotes are all that is left
of a race we once conquered

at night I hear them worshiping
gods with unspeakable names

I have learned to make use of pain
he never fails to take me
into his confidence telling me
more than I wanted to know

and when morning arrives bringing
whatever it can to help I ready myself
for the impetuous revival of sand

if I were to leave this desert
who would cherish transparent
light who would nurse broken stones
who would mother the cold

MY LOVE

when the crows fly away
with their compassion
and I remain to eat
whatever is left of my heart

I think of my love
with the odor of salt
of my love who holds me in her eyes
as if I were whole and beautiful

and I think of those
who walk the streets all night
frantic with desire and bruised
by the terrible small lips of rain

I touch you
as a blind man touches the dice
and finds he has won

SEVEN PRELUDES TO SILENCE

I

All day a wounded mountain followed me,
gentle and crumpled like a fern.
It was too shy to speak of its great need
and what could I have done to help it?

II

The desert has forgotten what it is waiting for.
Even sand will not survive without a purpose.
Can dust learn to swim? Will flowers
be able to repeat themselves in stone?

III

We have removed the earth's flesh and torn out
its bleeding veins. Sunlight reflects
from our knives. It blisters the surface
of the lake where nebulae of fish will never
return. A few gulls carry their white grief
on delicate hollow bones from water to water.

IV

We have forgotten that once there were black
swans with brilliant red beaks and curly
tail feathers. Soon the last birds of desperate
passage will ricochet through our oily rooms.

V

The stars confirm nothing, deny nothing. Heads
of animals grow on our walls. Their hopeless
glass eyes stare down at us without reproach.

VI

We who invented the clock and the metronome
cannot keep the calendar alive. We exist,
not on the edge of life but at its limits,
asking no pardon of the grass or the empty
shells which arrive and depart on each tide.

VII

In the book of our history it will be recorded
that we murdered the earth. With the name
of a different crime tattooed on each finger
we walk out into the orchard and find
tiny mirrors hanging from the trees. Listen.
The leaves are screaming for help as they fall.

REQUIEM FOR SONORA

I

a small child of a wind
stumbles toward me down the arroyo
lost and carrying no light
tearing its sleeves
on thorns of the paloverde
talking to itself
and to the dark shapes it touches
searching for what it has not lost
and will never find
searching
and lonelier
than even I can imagine

the moon sleeps
with her head on the buttocks of a young hill
and you lie before me
under moonlight as if under water
oh my desert
the coolness of your face

II

men are coming inland to you
soon they will make you the last resort
for tourists who have
nowhere else to go

what will become of the coyote
with eyes of topaz
moving silently to his undoing
the ocotillo

flagellant of the wind
the deer climbing with dignity
further into the mountains
the huge and delicate saguaro

what will become of those who cannot learn
the terrible knowledge of cities

III
years ago I came to you as a stranger
and have never been worthy
to be called your lover or to speak your name
loveliest
most silent sanctuary
more fragile than forests
more beautiful than water

I am older and uglier
and full of the knowledge
that I do not belong to beauty
and beauty does not belong to me
I have learned to accept
whatever men choose to give me
or whatever they choose to withhold
but oh my desert
yours is the only death I cannot bear

Vern Rutsala
(1934-   )

OTHER LIVES

You see them from train windows
in little towns, in those solitary lights
all across Nebraska, in the mysteries
of backyards outside cities—

a single face looking up,
blurred and still as a photograph.
They come to life quickly
in gas stations, overheard in diners,

loom and dwindle, families
from dreams like memories too
far back to hold. Driving by
you go out to all those strange

rooms, all those drawn shades,
those huddled taverns on the highway,
cars nosed-in so close they seem
to touch. And they always snap shut,

fall into the past forever, vast lives
over in an instant. You feed
on this shortness, this mystery
of nearness and regret—such lives

so brief you seem immortal;
and you feed, too, on that old hope—
dim as a half-remembered
phone number—that somewhere

people are as you were always
told they were—people who swim
in certainty, who believe, who age
with precision, growing gray like

actors in a high school play.

IN THE MIDDLE

Darkness let go of hills
then turned to mist
and snow dust on those
great humped backs
that brood over Indian
graves and secret springs.

You walked the other
way on sentences like
planks, exploring faces,
the life below surfaces.
And behind all that was
what you now have—

the evening. You look
at dandelions, heads
gray fuzz, and pick
them with watchmakers'
hands only to blow
them away, calling it

confetti for some future
small victory. But
it won't work. Somewhere
during the day you
were beaten, duped,
enrolled in madness;

but there are no signs—
only the spirit of a bruise
around you like smoke,
the ache of the flu
just before it happens,
thoughts like gnats,

nothing will settle.
It was speaking
and not speaking.
That and the razor
edges of hours
and cups, all those

calm minutes. Now
the voices of happiness
whisper, telling you
secrets about yourself
you did not know
and cannot believe.

The house is crowded
as a nightmare
and there are places
to go. You go to
those places. You
come back again.

THE JOURNEY BEGINS

Now they are loading the old Ford in the evening, taking too much luggage,
too much fried chicken in paper sacks, lost
even before leaving the muddy driveway.
With great care they jammed dirty shirts and underwear in the cracked
    suitcase,
everyone's clothes together, rank and wrinkled, the flanks
of the case already sprung, the lock losing its hold slowly.
Cardboard cartons filled with rusty towels, a half box of cereal,
the iron with the frayed cord go into the back seat
with army blankets and the squat thermos, spout dripping.

The old man sits very still on a kitchen chair while the women work.
His wife, near seventy, sighs and trembles
afraid of highway curves—blowouts hover on the road,
some vast clock figures collisions, fiery breakdowns coil
under the old car's hood. All afternoon she
travelled that long highway, conjuring each dangerous inch,
seeing guardrails spring open like gates
and the flimsy car soar and bounce down ravines
so deep no one has seen the bottom.

The old couple know only that their fat daughter has come
to rescue them from his sickness, its confusion, its haze
around them like woodsmoke.
She drove five hundred miles fueled by her mother's hysteria:
He was dying but still stumbled into town to drink,
swollen hands like mittens around a shot glass.
Drunk, he beat those big hands blue on the woodshed door.
Sober, he said the bar was there to keep him
from sitting like some old woman eating toothless bread and milk
with a baby's spoon hooked around his thumb.
He staggered home by moonlight, screaming through jackpine
for Bud and Ed, both dead twenty years,
to wake up and have a drink.
So his daughter—forty-five, three hundred pounds—
drove all night, losing count of flats,
splashing water to steam on the radiator.
Even now as they load the car she eats leftovers.
Her hands always seem greasy, the skin around her mouth glistens
and her lips shine as if she had just licked them
before having a picture taken.
You were always such a pretty girl, her mother says. So pretty.

The car sags with its burdens, mud high on the fenders like a watermark,
one headlight squinting blindly through the gloom.
The suitcase is now loosely tied on the trunk with clothesline—
the daughter counting more on balance than tension
in the line to hold it there. It is her way.
Springs lurch as they get in, the old man settling his brittleness
among blankets and boxes in the back.
Now fear of the road becomes worry over the house:
For the old woman every shingle becomes tinder,
every rafter flammable as balsa wood.

They set out in the dark along a dirt road, a blizzard of dust
around them from a passing logging truck.
Soon the old man sleeps.
His daughter counts his breaths in the rearview mirror.
The old woman winces at every branch that looms swiftly
like an enormous hawk above the car,
scrapes and thumps a claw once and is gone.
The car creeps and whines until they reach the cool blacktop,
suddenly free as skaters on the interstate.
But the wrong turn has waited patiently all day
and they take it gracefully, relaxing on the level road.
The old woman even hums and forgets fire.

They drive on, their lone map lost in a sack of fried chicken,
grease spots forming on it slowly, darkening the land.
Chainsmoking and swearing the daughter keeps steering north,
trying somehow to lean her bulk toward the West,
but the road refuses and they go on and on
as the dark smothers the car
and the blazing white hospital sheets recede with each
wheezing mile the old man breathes away.

LIKE THE POETS OF ANCIENT CHINA

We are captives now, prisoners of this
sad air, these terrible rugs,
these chairs that caress and hold,
these surfaces chosen like a new
skin. It's sea-level for us from now on.
Here we practice the cottage
industry of the banal; here we
probe the mysteries of the commonplace.
The work is steady, the pay poor.
But we move that way—bloodhounds
of memory, detectives of the ordinary,
explorers in seclusion. And something
always turns up, something to savor
on long winter nights—the ins
and outs of rumor, the intricate creases
of gossip that hint at some vast
answer if we could only find
the key. It keeps us busy chewing
until all the taste is gone
and it takes our minds off our
troubles too: we know the shadows
near us are alive, we know we're
prey. It's calm but we know
the night is armed. And true,
we live in the house of error
but we live, you see. There are
regions here no maps will ever mention;
there are legends, epics on the heads
of pins. Of course teeth grate
in closets and certainly cold hands
reach to us from drawers.
That's only the domestic gothic—
you have it too, a side-issue.
We're after bigger game. It responds
to nothing but our stillness.

PATHS

Walking alone on a strange street
I feel an old excitement,
a stirring like those car trips
in childhood that promised
another life, a new school
of echoes, the dull cargo
of the fool thrown overboard
for good: An old car climbs
the grade on Cabbage Hill
coughing steam, tires tender
as balloons. I remember
the knocking motor and all
around me the great silence
of held breath before we
breathed the icy summit's view.
The freight of memory
lumbers with me now down
all that twisting altitude.
My cardboard house folds up.
I am on the path again
that shows you how to lose.
Ozone's lost taste on the air,
no wind, no stir in the leaves
fears become eyes, an eye
for each weeping knothole,
eyes on my skin like kisses.
Once there were rumors
of dead grandfathers—muffled
voices in another room—
and whispers of others lost
in the woods, smothered bones
turned to twigs overnight.
I felt the force of the woods—
ferns winked starvation's eyes
and the cougar of the dark
padded close, huge yet so
delicate no twig broke.
The cat is always there

in the forest thick as sleep
near the path that leads
to cold kitchens. Deeper still
I remember the dirt road that led
to the old farm and how the car
bucked and rattled like a milktruck
over potholes, the farmhouse
rising and falling, pines dancing
the sky jagged. I waited
for the plank bridge. It seemed
only an armload of kindling
thrown over the ditch deep
with brown water, boards warped
and split thin as lath to
let us drown. But I knew
that if we fell it would be
farther, not just into brown water.
but farther, deeper, darker,
colder than water.

Lawson Fusao Inada
(1938-   )

ASIAN BROTHER, ASIAN SISTER

For Yoshiko Saito

I
Not yet dawn,
but the neighbors have been here,
bringing condolences, assurances
that my pupils will be seen to:

though I am new to their village
they include me, are grateful
for what I do.

The teacups are rinsed.
The bedding is stacked.
While my wife wraps our basket
the children kneel on the tatami,
fingering the beads of the rosary like an abacus.
In their way, they are hushed,
and seem to sense the solemnity.

"Sa. Iki-ma-sho."

A cold wind greets us.
There will be snow soon
in this prefecture.

Burnt wood, sweet fields.
Not yet dawn.
In one of these houses,
my grandmother is rising to go to school.

II
By sixteen,
she was in this country—

making a living, children
on the way.

I don't know what it cost
in passage, in the San Joaquin.

I'm beginning
to understand the conditions.

III
To get back to the source,
through doors

of dialects and restrictions . . .

Brazil to the south, this blue
shore on the horizon . . .

To get back to the source,
the need to leave

and bring it with you:

in 1912, they opened
the Fresno Fish Store.

IV
Ika, the squid,
to slither down your throat.

Saba, the mackerel,
to roast.

Maguro, the tuna—
slice it thin and raw.

Kani, the crab.
Awabi, the abalone.

All these
shipped in slick and shiney.

All these
to keep our seasons.

All these.

V
Grandmother never learned the language—
just a few
choice phrases to take care of business.
Grandfather ordered the fish.

But when the nice white man
bent down to her level and said
"How long you been here, Mama?"
she told him
"Come today fresh."

VI
Before the war, after
the old scrape of stench and scale,
she'd come to see what her new grandson could do.

Nine o'clock, but you've got to wake him,
so I can flip him in his crib.

Bring him down to the store tomorrow
so I can get him some manju,
let him chew on an ebi.

Part his hair in the middle,
slick it down,
so I can wheel him around to the people.

Listen, big baby—Mexican tunes
moving around the jukeboxes.
Listen, big fat round-headed baby in white shoes.

What chu mean
he's got small eyes?
What chu mean?
That's how he
supposed to be.
What chu mean?
Big fat baby in a hood.

In depths of bed,
to roll to where the shore was, undulating
coves and folds . . .

Drunks dancing wounded
under a wounded streetlight . . .

Then the Danish Creamery
screaming about its business
and we couldn't sleep.

Sing me. Sing me. Sing me
please about the pigeons
cooing home to the temple to roost.

Sing me. Please.

For our sweet tooth,
she kept a store
of canned fruit buried in the dirt
beside her barracks in Arkansas.

Water flopping over the furo's edges
as we entered, feet
sliding on slats,
a soft iceberg in the heat and steam . . .

So you've got a son in New Guinea,
another at some fort.
What do you do?
What have you *been* doing?—

try to keep busy and eat.

And as the children leave
to dicker with the enemy,
try to keep busy and eat.

Float around him,
bump and nudge him,
and try to keep busy and eat.

Shuffle off to the store
ten feet behind him
and try to keep busy and eat.

And when the sons take over,
try to keep busy and eat.

Go in and scream about the business.
Grandchildren stumbling
over their own skin in the suburbs,
hubcaps and money
cluttering the driveways . . .

One day they found her
flipping in a driveway like a fish.

If your hip is broken,
you can't ever go home—
roaming through Wakayama
for what the War didn't own.

If your hip is broken,
you can't ever go to Oregon.
You've got to wheel to your drawer
for your Issei medallion—

that steamer riding a starry-striped sea.

If your hip is broken,
you've got to give that medallion
with a moan—

as though you could know.

VII

My grandmother is in the beauty
of release.
As the heart subsides,
as the blood runs its course,
she is gowned and attended,
chanting incantations to Buddha.

I am touched by the beauty,
by the peace
that is the end of her life—

fluttering eyelids,
the mumuring barely audible.

It is goodbye.

It is beautiful.

I do not need to cry.

As the sheet flows over in its purity,
I note the smoothness
of skin, the grey-blue hair
echoed faintly over the lips.

Then the sheet becomes a paper bag,
and she slips out of that sack
off the kitchen table

and lands on her back
on the linoleum,

naked, moaning, the impact
having stunned her into fright.

And she grabs both legs of mine
and bends the knees
and brings me down upon her

blue mouth without teeth,
food beginning to swell
in her belly

where I am

crying, and not yet born.

VIII

This house. This house.
The paths become trenches to the telephone, the bathroom . . .
This house. The scent of Orient
and seven existences.
This house. The bedrooms
tacked-on then sealed-off
as each moved to the colonies.

This house. Fifty years in this house.
Lie in front of the heater and dream,
flames eating the snowflake
mica that shudder with color
like fish-scales—blue, red—dream . . .

Lie in front of this heater
and knead the pus
where fish-fins stuck,
your dreams a fish
wilting over this heater . . .

This house. Creamery and cleavers
going at each other down the wintery street.

Bitches in alleys,
bottles in dreams . . .

Who knew the black whore in the alley
of this house—
dead a week, wrapped in leaves . . .

Tread lightly in this house.
Appliances try the edge of trenches.
Grandchildren balance on the shelves—
tassled
offspring of another culture . . .

This house. The basement
crammed with ballast—
dolls, kimonoes, swords . . .

This house. That survived the War
and got stoned.
This house. Exhausted fumes

gnawing the garden on the shore.

In the mist of that shore,
the chrysanthemum
droops and nods.

This house.

It drops into the freeway
and I drown.

IX
Then the doors burst open
and the people come flooding in—

from all over the San Joaquin
come to form the procession.

There is a trench to the temple.

When you are in that trench,
there is no room
for much movement:

all that you move from
comes in on you;
all that you do
is judged upon.

Trapped in the trench,
I am smothered in my people,
chanting in procession to the temple.

And when we emerge in the temple
I am five feet two,
flat-faced, bent-legged, epicanthic
as I will ever be . . .

Do my eyes lie?

My people see I am beautiful.

Yes. I am rocked in the lap of Buddha.
Yes. Incense owns my clothes.
Yes. I am wrapped in beads.

Yes. My people.
Grandmother, take me in your arms.

What you say, I will do.

X
The procession continues . . .
My grandfather migrates
to my mother's house, in the suburbs.
Even the chrysanthemum
finds new root, in the suburbs.

I have the medallion
forever sailing on my breast—
a family and the seven gods of luck
in the hold.

Brothers, Sisters,
understand this:

you are in passage—
wherever you go
you are slanted
down to the bone.

Do your eyes lie?

Brothers, Sisters,
understand this:

you are beautiful.

And your beautiful grandmother
is dancing in your eyes,

cooing and cooing you
home to roost.

Primus St. John
(1939-   )

BIOLOGICAL LIGHT

We live here to eat;
Things stare at us.
Those things eat.
We call all of this hunger
The world.
Why?
Because we live here . . .

All over the world
Morning light is still happening
Like God.
It is so hard to tell
Who eats the plants first—
    Insect or crepuscular.

The wind feels the smallest birds
It's got.
If that is what we are,
It's not a lot—
Here comes the fox.

Noon: circles logically like the hawk.
God moves the rim around
Until the fox is in.
Now the fox is the hawk
And all the small things he ate
Believe him . . .

I have come here late;
The deer look like they have gone,
But thorns remind me
More is going on.

Gradually, memory sets the table back,
I have come from
Across the water, as far back
As I can know.
Friends there have eaten me;
Now I stand here, that torn by hate
As I myself have eaten them.

Late; the owls say whooo
For what more will surely come.
Finally, I am older—
But not enough—
Surrounded by what I know
Is falling back toward the grass
More like luck than hope . . .

I am just lying here
Thinking this in my sleep—
How cold it is outside.
If we were fish where it is very dark
It would all be so easy
Light would come from the dead things that we eat.

A SPLENDID THING GROWING

Chair:
It is the name of me.
The ending of my arms
And the ending of my legs
Mean nothing.
I cannot creak enough.

Dish:
It is the emptiness.
I am going to breathe
Over the edge,
And feel—
Louder.

Vase:
And water are righteousness.
So flowers are given,
So dance,
And wind
                within us.

Cup:
It is the round place.
So is intention.
So is our drinking.

Godliness:
That is knife.
Given decision.
Given harshness
                like cut.

Table:
Be with me
On this earth
It is set with our flesh.

Come closer:
Like carpet
And trust.
Dust in us
Everything woven.

Drapes:
They are disturbances,
And thinking.
Flapping makes no sense,
But storms.

Doom:
It is always left.
At night,
It is a splendid thing growing.
It shows us nothing.
Oh Nouns ! Forgive us.

ALL THE WAY HOME

The lamps hung like a lynching
In my town.
It was a dark town.
In a dark town,
Light is a ragged scar.
Fright begs that ragged scar.
It begs doorways.

I love that town.
From its lean men
I learned
Emotion;
And how to hold that fine edge,
That makes us
                people . . .

Mrs. Blackwell's
Sold her house.
Since her husband revolved his head,
She wears bright hats
That speak to people.

B.J.'s doing time.
His children betray that time,
By the breathing it takes
To dream through windows.
Mary Lee dreams him letters;
She dreams by heart . . .

Now I feel a new scar.
I've left home
And leaned so far,
I'm almost zero.
And though it's lonely
Whatever knowing is;
It strings a long fine wire.
At night I lie awake
And listen to that wire—

All the way home.

A POEM TO MY NOTEBOOK, ACROSS WINTER

The flock of birds takes shape
        If there is faith . . .
in the world, today
It is scattered, and the space
is lonely,
high up there, and cold.
        The leader,
I am afraid of these birds
Thumps for things . . .
this is hope   or
it is not a poem.
The tradition keeps flapping,
        wrong,
across the sun,
obtrusively like an author's intervention.
It's incomplete, rich experience,
but the best tip yet is dipping,
then diving, deep to the left . . .
        I hope

Peter Wild
(1940-   )

STEAKBONES

My neighbor puts steakbones
under his trees.
walking in the alley, there he is
this bishop of the church in his robe
and slippers, holding a lamp
like the sage on Hills Brothers Coffee
stooping, turning them over with a rake
because they are growing hair.
he spends evenings dozing
on the back porch chasing the dogs away
that sail back and forth over the fence.
on weekends lets his grandchildren
play with them, use them as boomerangs,
as parts for their airplanes. but when
they go home he makes them put them back
each to its own rounded place,
rotting eggs into their nests, like
loaded pistols back into their cases. I have read
that after years if the mice don't get them,
the ants carry them away, they begin to disintegrate,
a constant phosphorous rain like uranium
penetrating the soil. meanwhile they lie there
in their wild beards, some with lipstick smiles
on their faces, others growing the thin vestigial
legs of lizards, glowing in their circles,
humming their own private music
as above the citrus leaves curl turning a violent green
putting out their globing fruit, and he
lies awake on his back beneath his vandyke,
ripening overnight in anticipation.

A PASSING ILLNESS

Those good citizens the clouds
    go over without sickness,
  frogstroking toward their dreams
      with a passionless health.
and you having risen
    pale from your death at the proper hour
  to do the shopping, to send the dirt of our wash
      sucking through the city's system—
hearing the cars go by all day
    I throw off a week of books,
  stand out by the woodpile in the sun
      with my wool cap on
    slicing the logs into shadows.
    the axe falls, a bit of sunlight through my hands.
and you come home like a Lazarus
      not knowing the difference,
    tidy up the house.
that night the guests
    mumble like fathers in the next room
      talking about their children,
later come in a group to stand around
    the bed with sweating iridescent faces
    and mouths that tear when they whisper.

THE INDIANS

The trumpets blow
and Columbus stands on his island
the blue back of a tortoise
waving his reed sword
inviting the Indians to come ashore.
they advance stooped over, smiling,
bacon dripping from their lips, turning more red.
he lets them examine him, plunging
their hands through the holes, offers
them a model of the ship they came in.
they offer him baubles which he
inspects to be polite, then puts aside.

he notices the island is small and sinking
but invites them into his tent, the
size of an envelope. inside the hall
is paved with Bibles; they smoke
and call the terms back and forth.
finally the warriors outside rush in and bear him off
on their shoulders like a wooden corpse.
not used to such speed he watches the
clouds above and asks an assistant
for the latest messages from the king. at
camp they marry him off to their
most intelligent princess, let
him keep his notebooks and pistols. he spends
the rest of his life growing a moustache,
drunk in a blanket, squints at his children
running off over the hills like red
ants to conquer the world.

THE HORSE

Whenever the sheets are out
he can be found in his glass house
banging the piano with a taco,
the top of his head pulled back like the visor
of a helmet. smoke pours out of his mouth.
stamps his hooves on the pedals
singing, watching the blue girl
in her bottle flutter, flutter up on the shelf.
over the brush and sand dunes
over the distant litmus mountains
the fuses begin going off behind his cerebellum,
all around in the dry afternoon.
he looks down and he has a crinoline dress on
his maps begin jumping, spreading into the walls;
the music sticks to the end of his nose.
and as she goes faster, as her tail glows, splits,
snow and an ash fill the room,
he rears back, howls; a train
puffs out of the swamp, like a snake,
encircles the house. above
him his beer begins to boil.

DOG HOSPITAL

Riding by there every day
surrounded by eucalyptuses and palms
I hear them barking behind the whitewashed adobe fence,
see from my bicycle the ladies going in carrying
the loved ones in their arms—
in fact have been there myself
met the receptionist smiling beneath her cap,
read the magazines on training waiting
for the nodding Japanese man
who tries to pet her as he gives her shots,
gets bitten on the hand. nevertheless
days later she comes out smiling, refreshed
as she jumps into my arms and he almost
bowing winks. though riding by now
there are stories of those others calling
over the walls, that they are left to starve,
given other brains, arms
sewn to their necks, and
some are locked in canisters,
lowered down polished tubes
into caves where there is no light
except the candle in their heads,
and the shadows around them that they
seeing now bark at.

James Welch
(1940-)

ACROSS TO THE PELOPONNESE

The last decent man alive
died today in Saronis.
No one remembers what he did
or how he came to be so good.

He died today at ten past three,
the final tick of the soccer match.
Shepherds complained of a winter wind,
the butcher laid down his lamb.

Some mothers say he wrote poems,
stunning poems on rare paper
about . . . you see, they can't be sure,
the man was sadly foreign.

Flies walk against the windowpane.
A dog barks. So sure of itself
the Aegean mocks these mourners
gathered in his room.

Nobody knows how he died
or why—he had no enemies,
no friends, no murderous need
to throw himself against the rocks.

Fishermen light their nets
crude against the Peloponnese.
In Saronis the men are certain
Greece beat themselves, not the Turks.

WHY I DIDN'T GO TO DELPHI

My feet taste funny
in this light.
Flowers tell me nothing.
Was it all a dream,
a morning made by birds
sailing to Glyfada, dodging
caiques, red breezes
north from Africa?

Nikos drove that wet sea
wild with explanations
of demotic songs, Count Basie,
goat feet tender to the cliff.

I believed that slapstick chin,
old gestures of disdain,
older gestures of the knife
slicing off that final breath
of fifteen-day-old lambs.

The butcher looked up,
startled. His mother
brought a basin of water.
Reflected off Hymettus,
the sea changed to asphodel.
Children who could not speak
spoke, and that sad oracle
wild with premonition,
for the seventh time
explained the origin of death.

SNOW COUNTRY WEAVERS

A time to tell you things are well.
Birds flew south a year ago.
One returned, a blue-wing teal
wild with news of his mother's love.

Mention me to friends. Say
wolves are dying at my door,
the winter drives them from their meat.
Say this: say in my mind

I saw your spiders weaving threads
to bandage up the day. And more,
those webs were filled with words
that tumbled meaning into wind.

IN MY FIRST HARD SPRINGTIME

Those red men you offended were my brothers.
Town drinkers, Buckles Pipe, Star Boy,
Billy Fox, were blood to bison. Albert Heavy Runner
was never civic. You are white and common.

Record trout in Willow Creek chose me
to deify. My horse, Centaur, part cayuse,
was fast and mad and black. Dandy in flat hat
and buckskin, I rode the town and called it mine.

A slow hot wind tumbled dust against my door.
Fed and fair, you mocked my philosophic nose,
my badger hair. I rolled your deference
in the hay and named it love and lasting.

Starved to visions, famous cronies top Mount Chief
for names to give respect to Blackfeet streets.
I could deny them in my first hard springtime,
but choose amazed to ride you down with hunger.

CALL TO ARMS

We spoke like public saints
to the people assembled in the square.
Our gestures swayed the morning light
and bathed the town in public guilt.

All the weather poured down that hour
our lips witched the ears of thousands.
Whiny kids broke from their mothers' arms,
charged the fields, armed with sticks.

Men wept and women clutched their steaming
heads and beat the savage mildness
from their hearts. The eyes were with us,
every one, and we were with the storm.

We road out that night, our ponchos slick
and battered down against our thighs.
Our horses knew the way. None looked behind,
but heard the mindless suck of savage booted feet.

CHRISTMAS COMES TO MOCCASIN FLAT

Christmas comes like this: Wise men
unhurried, candles bought on credit (poor price
for calves), warriors face down in wine sleep.
Winds cheat to pull heat from smoke.

Friends sit in chinked cabins, stare out
plastic windows and wait for commodities.
Charlie Blackbird, twenty miles from church
and bar, stabs his fire with flint.

When drunks drain radiators for love
or need, chiefs eat snow and talk of change,
an urge to laugh pounding their ribs.
Elk play games in high country.

Medicine Woman, clay pipe and twist tobacco,
calls each blizzard by name and predicts
five o'clock by spitting at her television.
Children lean into her breath to beg a story:

Something about honor and passion,
warriors back with meat and song,
a peculiar evening star, quick vision of birth.
Blackbird feeds his fire. Outside, a quick 30 below.

GRAVELY

we watched her go the way she came,
unenvied, wild—cold as last spring rain.
Mule deer browsed her garden down
to labored earth, seed and clean carrots.

Dusk is never easy, yet she took it
like her plastic saint, grandly, the day
we cut those morning glories down
and divvied up her odds and ends.

Daughters burned sheets the following Monday.
All over God's city, the high white stars
welcomed her the way she'd planned: a chilly
satellite ringing round the great malicious moon.

215

Sandra McPherson
(1943-   )

ELEGIES FOR THE HOT SEASON

1. The Killing of the Snails

Half the year has hot nights, like this,
When gnats fly thick as stars, when the temperature is taken
On the tongues of flowers and lovers,
When the just-dead is buried in warm sod.
The snail-pebbled lawns glimmer with slime trails, and the unworried,
Unhurried snail tucks into his dark knuckle, stockaded
With spears of grass, safe. When I first heard
The sound of his dying, it was like knuckles cracking.

The lightest foot can slay snails. Their shells break
More easily than mirrors. And like bad luck, like
A face in a mirror, they always come back.

Good hunting nights were stuffy as a closed room.
No moon shone but my father's flashlight.
As if it were Jericho, he circled the house,
And I'd hear all evening the thick crunch
Of his marching, the sound of death due
To his size 13 shoe.

In the morning I'd find them little clots on the grass, pretend
They'd been singed by geranium fire-bursts, asphyxiated by blue
Iris flame, burnt to shadows under the strawberry blossom.
The fuchsias bled for them. White-throated calla lilies
Maintained appearances above the snail slum.

But the slow-brained pests forgave and fragilely claimed the garden
The next hot season, like old friends, or avengers.

2. The Killing of the Caterpillars

Today I watch our neighbor celebrating May,
Ringing round the besieged cherry-tree,
His haunted maypole, brandishing his arson's torch
Through the tents of caterpillars. He plays conductor,
Striking his baton for the May music.
And the soft, fingery caterpillars perform,
Snap, crackle, pop.

They plummet through a holiday of leaves like fireworks or shooting stars or
    votive candles
Or buttercups, under the hex of the neighbor's wand, first fruits of
    euthanasia,
Ripe and red before the cherries. And it is over,
Grown cold as a sunset. They lie on the grass
Still and black as those who lie under it.

It is night. Lights burn in the city
Like lamps of a search-party, like the search-beam
Of my father's flashlight, at every swing discovering
Death.

PREPARATION

It was likely to occur during the happiest story
Or at the explosion of a brainstorm or as the product fused
From mere numbers. The blue sky we knew would go
Yellow and fearsick, then after the flash, white

As a bloodless Caucasian. What we had to learn was like dancing:
To follow. A desk, no protection from the teacher's C,
Would save our lives. There were times we wondered—would we
Go all at once, tightly curled little foetuses, roomsful

Of legal abortions? A brace of peace
Holding our shoulders back bent. We were suspicious
Of white dawns. We kept one ear ready always
For the voice of our siren mother.

We expect now the friendly alarm Wednesdays
As Sundays we depend on brimstone to quake the church.
Some say that God alone, though he doesn't laugh, is not scared. And that
There still are those who sing without government like birds

And are prepared.

WEARING WHITE

The old dogged ways of writing poems
Cover with snow. Juncoes, bodied like lynx tails,
Fly out of the empty prison.

Dipping his hand in blood the taxidermist complains
Nothing will stay on this white. He raises
A frozen wasp by a leg, beginning to move.

On maples the sensory tips say: we refuse,
Not another experiment. They wonder if they are not
Warped by feeling. Frosting the interior

That faces them a pocket watch hangs, stopped
And silver. It listens as the leaves clatter
Into glassy cornerings. An idea

Of what to do with an idea: I am wearing white—
The height of the heart of a tree in my boreal
Cloths. My seamstress sets down

Her needle, with a headache. Like windows
Painted shut, snow everywhere hardens. My hands
Are cold, and they must keep cold, like milk.

Notes on the Contributors by Howard Robinson

Earle Birney was born in Alberta, Canada, and has studied in British Columbia, London, and California. He is currently professor of English and writer in residence at the University of Toronto. A world traveler, he has lectured and taught in such diverse places as Japan, India, New Zealand, Australia, and South America. His poetry (see *Selected Poems,* 1940-1966) has been called the product of "a wilder Chaucer," "zestful," "genial," and "gritty [with] realism." In addition to his poems, he has also written several novels and plays.

J. V. Cunningham has been rated as "the most consistently distinguished poet writing in English today, and one of the finest in the language" (Yvor Winters). Although Cunningham has not published a large amount of poetry, the quality of his work is consistently high. He is at present professor of English at Brandeis, having taught at Stanford, the University of Hawaii, the University of Chicago, and the University of Virginia. He has won several awards for his poetry, including a Guggenheim fellowship, and is also an author of several critical studies.

Madeline De Frees (formerly Sister Mary Gilbert) teaches in the writing program at the University of Montana, where she has been professor of English since 1967. Before that she taught at various colleges in the northwest, principally those conducted by the Sisters of the Holy Names, an order to which she belonged until 1973. In 1965 she was Writer-in-Residence at Seattle University, and in fall 1974 was a visitor to the creative writing faculty of the University of Victoria. Her work has appeared in numerous anthologies and magazines, and her second collection of poems is due from Braziller in 1975.

Thomas Hornsby Ferril has lived all his life in his native Denver where he has been employed in industry and as an editor of the *Rocky Mountain Herald.* He has authored five volumes of verse, a collection of essays, and several plays. Though he is highly respected for his concrete depiction of the mountains, prairies, and seasons, his poetry always concerns living man. His numerous awards include winning the Yale Younger Poets competition, the Oscar Blumenthal prize, *The Nation's* poetry prize, the Central City (Colorado) Opera House award, and awards from the Academy of American Poets, the Poetry Society of America, and the Colorado Council of Arts and Humanities.

Brewster Ghiselin, between 1934 and his recent retirement, was a member of the faculty of the University of Utah, where he implemented the creative writing program and directed it for many years. He has published his work in most of the leading journals and magazines around the country, and is the author of three volumes of verse. He has received several awards for his poems, among them a grant from the National Institute of Arts and Letters. In addition to his poetry, he has also made important contributions as critic and editor (see *The Creative Process*).

Thom Gunn is from England, but has spent most of his career in this country as student, teacher, and writer. After graduate work at Cambridge and at Stanford, he became associate professor of English at the University of California at Berkeley. In 1966, however, he left the academic life to become a writer on a full-time basis, and at present continues to produce a considerable amount of poetry and criticism. He has authored half a dozen books of poetry (see *Selected Poems,* 1962), and has received the Levinson prize, the Somerset Maugham award, and a grant from the National Institute of Arts and Letters.

John Haines started his creative career as a painter and sculptor, but later turned to the writing of poetry. His life has been punctuated by a series of miscellaneous jobs—clerk, carpenter, fisherman—and for a brief time he worked for the Department of the Navy in Washington, D.C. He eventually moved with his family to Alaska, where for several years he spent his time homesteading, and writing what the critics have called "concrete, surrealistic, grave" poetry, which often deals with the theme of death. In 1965-66 he received a Guggenheim fellowship. At present he teaches English at the University of Washington.

Kenneth O. Hanson received his B.A. at the University of Idaho and studied Chinese language and comparative literature at the University of Washington. At present he is a professor of literature at Reed College in Portland, Oregon. He is the author of three collections of poetry and has received many awards, notably Fulbright and Rockefeller fellowships, a Bollingen grant, Lamont and Theodore Roethke awards, and an Amy Lowell Traveling Poetry scholarship.

John Sterling Harris was raised in Tooele, Utah, and educated at the University of Utah, Brigham Young University, and the University of Texas. He currently teaches American literature and technical writing at Brigham Young University, and has also taught at the University of Texas and Bowling Green State University of Ohio. He has published widely as a technical writer on firearms, on technical writing theory, and on pedagogy. Besides his book of poems, *Barbed Wire* (1974), he is coauthor of the forthcoming *Technical Writing for the Social Sciences.* He is national president of the Association of Teachers of Technical Writing.

Richard Hugo, after receiving B.A. and M.A. degrees from the University of Washington, spent thirteen years as an industrial writer for Boeing Aircraft. Turning to the writing of poetry, he was recognized twice in 1965, with the Pacific Northwest Booksellers award and the Northwest Writers book of the year award. He also received a Rockefeller Foundation grant in 1967, with which he spent a year abroad. He has taught at the University of Montana and is currently a faculty member at the University of Colorado. His work has been seen in many journals and magazines in recent years and he is the author of three books of poetry.

Lawson Fusao Inada has indicated that his current interest is "the creation and discovery of Asian-American culture. I have always been involved with Third World culture." His work as both poet and editor reflects these concerns: he is the author of several volumes of poems and is coeditor of a recent anthology, *Aiiieeeee!: Asian American Writing.* He is at present an associate professor of English at Southern Oregon College, having taught previously at the University of New Hampshire and at Lewis and Clark College.

Robinson Jeffers, one of the more widely known poets in this volume, spent nearly all of his life near the coastal town of Carmel, California. After graduation from Occidental College he began a career in medicine, but soon left it in order to devote his full time to poetry. He is author of a score of books, most of which exemplify his particular skill with the longer narrative forms. His work, which at times is harsh and negative in effect, has nevertheless secured him a position among the finest poets of the twentieth century.

Clinton F. Larson's poems have been widely anthologized in magazines and literary journals, and he has published several volumes of verse (see *The Lord of Experience and Counterpoint*). His special forte is the poetic drama; he has written over thirty works for the stage, many of which have been performed numerous times. He took his Ph.D. at the University of Denver, and is at present professor of English and Poet in Residence at Brigham Young University.

Philip Levine holds an M.A. degree in English from Wayne State University. He is the author of eight books of poetry and has contributed to numerous magazines and journals. He has been awarded the Stanford poetry fellowship, the Joseph Henry Jackson award, the Chaplebrook Foundation award, a Guggenheim fellowship, and a grant from the National Endowment for the Arts. His most recent book of poetry is *1933* (1974). He is currently a member of the faculty at Fresno State College.

Edward Lueders received his Ph.D. from the University of New Mexico in 1952 and then remained as a member of the faculty for several years, teaching both English and speech. Later he became associate professor of English at Long Beach State College, and is at present professor of English at the University of Utah. He is widely known as an editor and critic and has published his work in several journals and magazines. In addition to his literary pursuits he is also an accomplished jazz pianist.

Sandra McPherson was educated at San Jose State College and at the University of Washington, and then spent one year as a technical writer in an industrial corporation. She has published her poetry in some twenty periodicals, and two collections of her work are available: *Elegies for the Hot Season* (1974) and *Radiation* (1973). She has received the Helen Bullis prize, an Ingram Merrill grant, and an award from the National Council on the Arts. At present she conducts workshops and poetry readings in the Portland area and nationally.

Josephine Miles has been professor of English at the University of California, Berkeley, since 1940. For her poetry (see *Poems,* 1930-1960) she has received the Phelan award, the Shelley award, a Guggenheim fellowship, the Blumenthal prize, and awards from both the National Institute of Arts and Letters and the National Endowment for the Arts. "My main hope for poetry," she writes, "is that it gets back into public use . . . that it becomes recitable, quotable, usable by everybody." She is also an editor and scholar, having produced dozens of books and articles dealing with many phases of English and American literature.

Veneta Nielsen received her degrees at Utah State University where she remained as faculty member, conducting classes in poetry appreciation and creative writing. She has published three volumes of verse: *Under Sound, Tree of Fire,* and *Insurgent Form,* as well as a textbook, *To Find the Poem,* which is used at Utah State and other schools in poetry classes. In addition to her academic duties, she at present spends much of her time as a lecturer for workshops and literary clubs.

Anthony Ostroff did graduate work at both the Sorbonne in Paris and the University of Grenoble after receiving his M.A. from the University of Michigan. Much of his teaching career has been spent at Berkeley, where from 1949 to 1969 he was professor of speech, although for short periods he has also taught at both Vassar and the University of Buffalo. He has earned a Fulbright fellowship and the Robert Frost fellowship for his poetry and is also an accomplished writer of fiction. He has lived and traveled in France and Mexico. He is currently professor of English at Lewis and Clark College.

Kenneth Rexroth's variegated career has included a number of miscellaneous jobs—including manual laborer and insane asylum attendant—and a diverse schooling, which he refers to as his "self-education." He is the recipient of several awards for his poetry (see *New and Selected Poems,* 1963), among them the Shelley Memorial award, an Amy Lowell fellowship, and a Guggenheim fellowship. In addition to his poetry he is an editor and critic of merit, and the author of several volumes of essays. His work has been called "humanistic," "witty," and "at times, difficult." He is now regarded as one of the foremost abstract painters in the country, having displayed his works in several one-man showings.

Theodore Roethke is another of those in this volume whose reputation is secure as one of the few great modern poets. He was awarded virtually all of the major laurels of the profession. In addition to a Bollingen prize and an Edna St. Vincent Millay award, he won a Pulitzer prize (1953) and two National Book awards (1958 and 1965, the latter awarded posthumously). He was born in Michigan in 1908 and had a long career as a teacher at numerous institutions. He taught for many years at the University of Washington until his death in 1963. Since then, Roethke's poetry has increased in importance and has been the subject of many critical works. The definitive edition of his poems is *The Collected Poems of Theodore Roethke,* 1966.

Vern Rutsala has been characterized as being a poet with "one of the keenest poetic senses of contemporary society," whose poetry is "an incredible illumination of the things that are so ordinary that we have forgotten them" (Norman Friedman). Rutsala has published several books of poetry and has been included in many important contemporary anthologies. He is a graduate of the State University of Iowa writing program (MFA), and is currently an associate professor of English at Lewis and Clark College. He recently received the NEA writing fellowship, 1974-75. *Laments,* a volume of his poetry, will soon be available.

Primus St. John is currently an assistant professor of English at Portland State College and formerly was poet in residence in a Tacoma Public Schools program. He has published his work in several magazines and literary journals and was recently included in Harper and Row's *Poetry of Black America*. In addition to his academic work, he has been employed in a number of miscellaneous positions including laborer and postal clerk.

Ralph Salisbury received an MFA degree from the State University of Iowa and has won awards for both poetry and fiction. He is at present a professor of English at the University of Oregon, where he has taught since 1960. He has so far written one book of poetry, *Ghost Grapefruit.* He won a Chaplebrook Foundation award in 1966. He continues to write poetry and fiction, and his work has been published in many of the major magazines and journals.

Karl Shapiro was born in Baltimore and educated at Johns Hopkins, but has spent most of his teaching career at the universities of Nebraska, Indiana, and California (Berkeley and Davis). He is the recipient of most of the well-known awards, notably a Pulitzer prize (*V-Letter and Other Poems,* 1945), two Guggenheim fellowships, and the Bollingen prize for poetry (1969). He is the author of no less than twenty volumes of poetry and criticism and has contributed to most of the major journals and magazines. He is highly critical of modern poetry, feeling that its status as "the most ignored of the arts" is, quite possibly, justified.

Richard Shelton taught in the Arizona public schools for several years before enrolling for graduate work at the University of Arizona, where he eventually became instructor and associate professor of English. In addition to his contributions to various journals and magazines, he has produced six books of poetry (see *Of All the Dirty Words,* 1973). In 1970 he received the International Poetry Forum's United States award.

Clarice Short was born in 1910 at Ellinwood, Kansas, and after taking a Ph.D. at Cornell (1941), taught for several years at Fort Hays, Kansas State College. In 1946 she joined the faculty of the University of Utah, where she is at present professor of English. She is a current member of numerous professional organizations and was recently president of the Rocky Mountain Modern Language Association. Her work (see *The Old One and the Wind,* 1973) is highly regarded. She is also the author of several critical works which deal with romantic and Victorian poetry.

Robin Skelton was born in England in 1925, but has spent much of his life teaching in the United States and Canada. He is at present chairman of the department of creative writing at the University of Victoria, British Columbia. He has written several volumes of poetry and is also highly regarded as a critic, having produced books on Synge, Edward Thomas, and others. He received his degrees from the University of Leeds in England.

Gary Snyder was born in San Francisco in 1930, and although at present he lives in a rural area of Northern California, he has often been associated with the important San Francisco literary movements of the fifties and sixties. Snyder's reputation has grown considerably in recent years, and he is generally regarded as the most influential and articulate poet of his generation. The diversity in his work is perhaps due to a wide array of poetic mentors, including Tu Fu, Archilochus, Mila Repa, Blake, Jeffers, Whitman, Pound, Williams, and "the unknown Makers of devotional Tantric Songs." He has received numerous awards for his work, which has been widely anthologized.

Radcliffe Squires was born in Salt Lake City but spent most of his career at Harvard, Dartmouth, and the University of Michigan, where he has been a professor of English since 1952. He has published his work in many prominent journals and has produced three books of poetry: *Waiting in the Bone*, 1973; *Light Under Islands*, 1967; and *Fingers of Hermes*, 1965. Also known as a literary critic, he has written perceptively on Jeffers, Frost, Prokosch, and others. In 1959-60 he was a Fulbright lecturer in Greece.

William Stafford was born in Hutchinson, Kansas, and received his degrees at the University of Kansas and at Iowa State University. Though he has taught at Manchester College and at San Jose State College, most of his teaching career has been spent at Lewis and Clark. In addition to his several volumes of verse, he also writes prose (*Down in My Heart,* regarding his experiences as a conscientious objector; and *The Voices of Prose,* a textbook). He won the National Book Award in 1963 (*Traveling through the Dark*) and has earned numerous other awards, including the Shelley Award, a Danforth Foundation grant, and a Guggenheim grant.

Ann Stanford has taught both journalism and English and was for some years poetry reviewer for the *Los Angeles Times.* At present she is professor of English at California State University, Northridge. She is the author of several books of poetry, among them the prize-winning *Magellan: A Poem to Be*

Read by Several Voices. Her poems have appeared in many anthologies, and were included in *Best Poems* (Borestone Awards) virtually every year from 1959 to 1973.

A. Wilber Stevens studied at Brown University (A.B.) and the University of Washington (M.A. and Ph.D.). He has taught at numerous colleges and universities, and is presently dean of the College of Arts and Letters and professor of English at the University of Nevada at Las Vegas. His travels include Fulbright professorships in Burma, Thailand, and Brazil. His best-known poetic publication is *Pocatello* (1964). His other works include *Poems Southwest* and *Stories Southwest.* He edited and published the well-known literary magazine *Interim* for many years. He has written on such topics as poetic tragedy, George Orwell, F. Scott Fitzgerald, and literary ecology. He continues to review drama and music for various newspapers in the United States and to work as a teacher, dean, actor, and writer. His published poems are being prepared for book publication.

May Swenson was born in Logan, Utah, and although she has lived in New York since 1949 the "western" influence is evident in many of her poems. She is widely published in anthologies and is the author of several volumes of verse (see *To Mix With Time, New and Selected Poems,* 1963; *Poems to Solve,* 1966; *Iconographs,* 1970). She has received a Guggenheim fellowship, a Rockefeller writing grant, the William Rose Benet prize, and a Ford Foundation grant. In 1968 she received the Distinguished Service Gold Medal from Utah State University and in 1970 was made a member of the National Institute of Arts and Letters. At present she works under a writing grant from the National Endowment for the Arts.

Emma Lou Thayne has taught creative writing at the University of Utah. Mrs. Thayne's poetry has appeared in many periodicals. She has published three collections of verse: *Spaces in the Sage,* (1971); *Until Another Day for Butterflies,* (1973); and *On Slim Unaccountable Bones* (1974). *With Love, Mother,* a collection of prose and poetry published by Deseret Book Company, and a novel, *Past the Gate,* Peregrine Smith, appeared in 1975.

David Wagoner is currently professor of English at the University of Washington, where he has been a member of the faculty since 1954. In recognition of his poetry, a representative collection of which is in his *New and Selected Poems,* he has received numerous awards, notably Guggenheim and Ford fellowships and an award from the National Institute of Arts and

Letters. In addition to his poetry he has achieved stature in fiction and drama: he is author of more than a dozen books which represent all three approaches to literature.

James Welch is one of several poets in this volume who have worked at odd jobs—forest service, ranch hand—while producing high quality poetry. His book of verse *Riding the Earthboy* was well-received, and he has published his work in several prominent magazines. In addition to his poetry he writes fiction, having recently published a novel. At present he is involved in a public school poetry program in Missoula, Montana.

Peter Wild was born in Northampton, Massachusetts, in 1940. After receiving his MFA at Irvine he began his teaching career in the West. He is particularly noted for his considerable output of work in just a few years. Since 1968 he has published over ten volumes of poetry (see *Dilemma,* 1971) and has won two prizes in national poetry contests. He has also been a recent recipient of the Hart Crane and Alice Crane Williams Memorial Fund award. At present he is an associate professor of English at the University of Arizona.

John Williams is at present professor of English at the University of Denver, where he has taught since 1954. He was also a member of the faculty at the University of Missouri, where he received his Ph.D. and was writer in residence at Smith College. For several years he has occupied a position as staff member for the Bread Loaf Writers' Conference. In addition to his two volumes of verse he has written four novels. He received a Rockefeller award for fiction and a grant from the National Endowment for the Arts. His recent novel, *Augustus,* received the National Book Award.

Keith Wilson has written several volumes of verse and has been highly regarded as a contributor to anthologies and journals. It has been said of his poetry that he "gives the feeling of the landscape of the Southwest, and of the sense of a man growing within that landscape"; and that implicit in his work is a concern for the three basic cultures of the area, "the Indian, the white American, and the Mexican, each with his own aura, and each the counterpart of the other." He is at present associate professor of English at New Mexico University, having spent some time during his career as a technical writer for an industrial corporation.

Yvor Winters was born and educated in Chicago, but owing to ill health was compelled to move to the drier climate of the Southwest. He eventually settled in California, becoming professor of English at Stanford University, where he remained until his death in 1968. He is highly regarded as an editor and as author of numerous critical works, the most influential of which, *In Defense of Reason,* deals with nineteenth- and twentieth-century verse. His poetry, which has been called "classical," has been widely anthologized. The *Collected Poems* were selected from a half dozen earlier volumes, and appeared in 1952.

Index

230

232